YORK NOTES

D0587804

AN INSPECTOR CALLS

J. B. PRIESTLEY

NOTES BY JOHN SCICLUNA
REVISED BY MARY GREEN

PEARSON

YORK
PRESS

YORK PRESS
322 Old Brompton Road, London SW5 9JH

PEARSON EDUCATION LIMITED
Edinburgh Gate, Harlow,
Essex CM20 2JE, United Kingdom
Associated companies, branches and representatives throughout the world

First published 1997
New editions 2002, 2010
This new and fully revised edition 2015

10 9

ISBN 978–1–4479–8216–6

Illustrations by Timo Grubing and Rob Foote (page 61 only)
Phototypeset by Carnegie Book Production
Printed in Slovakia by Neografia

Photo credits: David Muscroft/Shutterstock for page 8 middle / Phil Dickson/Thinkstock for page 9 middle / kuzina/Shutterstock for page 10 top / nameinfame/Thinkstock for page 13 bottom / Alastair Wallace/Shutterstock for page 16 bottom / © Uluc Ceylani/Shutterstock for page 17 bottom / Valdis torms/Shutterstock for page 19 middle / © Carlos Caetano/Shutterstock for page 20 bottom / chrisdorney/Shutterstock for page 21 bottom / Masson/Shutterstock for page 24 bottom right / Sandra Cunningham/Shutterstock for page 27 middle / David muscroft/Shutterstock for page 29 top / Snusmumr/Shutterstock for page 33 bottom / Fluke samed/Shutterstock for page 34 bottom / Steve Allen/Shutterstock for page 39 top / Mg7/Thinkstock for page 41 middle / Alistair Scott/Thinkstock for page 43 top / Underworld111/Thinkstock for page 44 bottom / Carolyn Franks/Shutterstock for page 45 bottom / Tim Graham/Alamy for page 46 bottom / aluxum/Shutterstock for page 47 middle / chrisbrignell/Shutterstock for page 48 middle / kittimages/Thinkstock for page 50 bottom / Maritije/ Shutterstock for page 51 bottom / Gemenacom/ Shutterstock for page 52 middle / Lisa S/ Shutterstock for page 55 bottom / © iStock/PK Photos for page 57 bottom / Sue C/ Shutterstock for page 59 middle / PunishDonhongsa/Thinkstock for page 63 bottom / © iStock/maxuser for page 65 top / Sasha/Hulton Archive/Getty Images for page 66 top/ Bloomua/Shutterstock for page 66 bottom / StudioSmart/ Shutterstock for page 68 middle / vavuzunlu/Shutterstock for page 70 bottom / wavebreakmedia/ Shutterstock for page 79 middle

CONTENTS

PREPARING FOR ASSESSMENT

HOW WILL I BE ASSESSED ON MY WORK ON *AN INSPECTOR CALLS*?

All exam boards are different but whichever course you are following, your work will be examined through these four Assessment Objectives:

Assessment Objectives	Wording	Worth thinking about …
AO1	Read, understand and respond to texts. Students should be able to: ● maintain a critical style and develop an informed personal response ● use textual references, including quotations, to support and illustrate interpretations.	● How well do I know what happens, what people say, do etc.? ● What do *I* think about the key ideas in the play? ● How can I support my viewpoint in a really convincing way? ● What are the best quotations to use and when should I use them?
AO2	Analyse the language, form and structure used by a writer to create meanings and effects, using relevant subject terminology where appropriate.	● What specific things does the writer 'do'? What choices has Priestley made (why this particular word, phrase or paragraph here? Why does this event happen at this point?) ● What effects do these choices create – suspense? Nervous laughter? Reflective mood?
AO3	Show understanding of the relationships between texts and the contexts in which they were written.	● What can I learn about society from the play? (What does it tell me about workers' rights in the 1910s, for example?) ● What was society like in Priestley's time? Can I see it reflected in the play?
AO4	Use a range of vocabulary and sentence structures for clarity, purpose and effect, with accurate spelling and punctuation.	● How accurately and clearly do I write? ● Are there small errors of grammar, spelling and punctuation I can get rid of?

Look out for the Assessment Objective labels throughout your York Notes Study Guide – these will help to focus your study and revision!

The text used in these notes is the Heinemann edition, 1992.

HOW TO USE YOUR YORK NOTES STUDY GUIDE

You are probably wondering what is the best and most efficient way to use your York Notes Study Guide on *An Inspector Calls*. Here are three possibilities:

A **step-by-step** study and revision guide	A **'dip-in' support** when you need it	A **revision guide** after you have finished the novel
Step 1: Read Part Two as you read the play, as a companion to help you study it. **Step 2:** When you need to, turn to Parts Three to Five to focus your learning. **Step 3:** Then, when you have finished, use Parts Six and Seven to hone your exam skills, revise and practise for the exam.	Perhaps you know the book quite well, but you want to check your understanding and practise your exam skills? Just look for the section you think you need most help with and go for it!	You might want to use the Notes after you have finished your study, using Parts Two to Five to check over what you have learned, and then work through Parts Six and Seven in the immediate weeks leading up to your exam.

HOW WILL THE GUIDE HELP YOU STUDY AND REVISE?

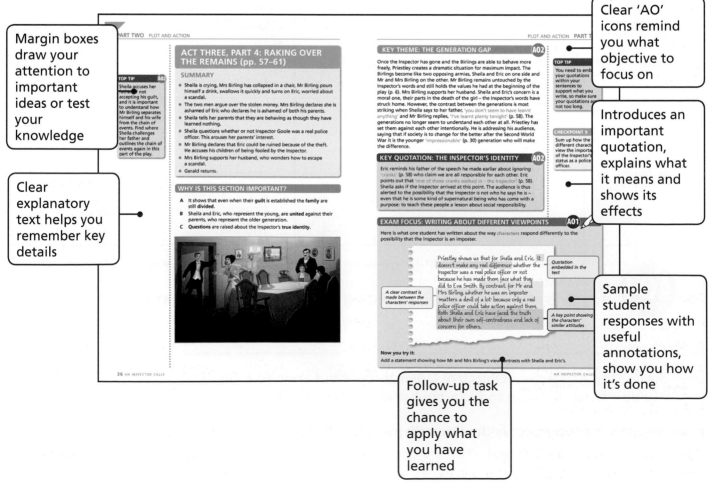

Margin boxes draw your attention to important ideas or test your knowledge

Clear explanatory text helps you remember key details

Clear 'AO' icons remind you what objective to focus on

Introduces an important quotation, explains what it means and shows its effects

Sample student responses with useful annotations, show you how it's done

Follow-up task gives you the chance to apply what you have learned

Themes are explained clearly with bullet-points which give you ideas you might use in your essay responses

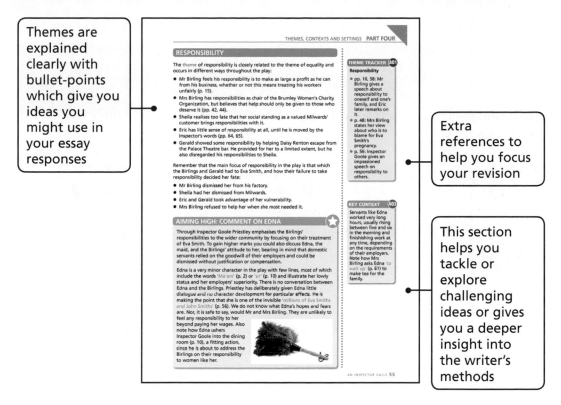

Extra references to help you focus your revision

This section helps you tackle or explore challenging ideas or gives you a deeper insight into the writer's methods

Finally, Parts Two to Five end with a **Progress and Revision Check**:

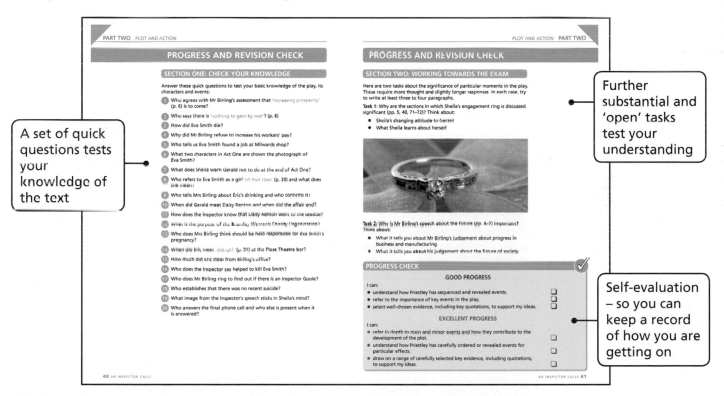

A set of quick questions tests your knowledge of the text

Further substantial and 'open' tasks test your understanding

Self-evaluation – so you can keep a record of how you are getting on

Don't forget Parts Six and Seven, with advice and practice on **improving your writing skills**:

- Focus on **difficult areas** such as **'context'** and **'inferences'**
- **Short snippets** of **other students' work** to show you how it's done (or not done!)
- Three annotated **sample responses** to a task **at different levels**, with **expert comments**, to help you judge your own level
- **Practice questions**
- **Answers** to the **Progress and Revision Checks** and **Checkpoint** margin boxes

Now it's up to you! Don't forget – there's even more help on our website with more sample answers, essay plan and even online tutorials. Go to www.yorknotes.com to find out more.

PLOT SUMMARY: WHAT HAPPENS IN *AN INSPECTOR CALLS*?

ACT ONE: MEETING THE CHARACTERS

- The Birling family and Gerald Croft are celebrating Sheila's engagement to Gerald.

- Mr Birling makes pompous speeches outlining his views on the advances in science, new inventions and the relationship between bosses and workers. He says they should ignore the 'cranks' (p. 10) who claim that everybody has a responsibility to care for everybody else.

- The evening is interrupted by the arrival of a police inspector named Goole making enquiries about the suicide of a young woman, Eva Smith.

- Shown a photograph of the girl, Mr Birling admits that he employed her in his factory but sacked her for being one of the leaders of a strike for higher wages.

- Sheila and Eric both feel that their father has acted harshly, while Gerald supports Mr Birling's claim that he acted reasonably.

- Sheila is shown the photograph and realises that, driven by jealousy and ill temper, she later had the girl sacked from her job as a shop assistant.

- When Gerald hears that the girl changed her name to Daisy Renton, his reaction shows that he too has known the girl.

- The Inspector suggests that many people share responsibility for the misery which prompted Eva Smith/Daisy Renton to end her life.

- Left alone with Gerald, Sheila warns him not to try to hide anything from the Inspector.

KEY CONTEXT

Women's wages were lower than men's in the Edwardian period, so the Inspector's comment that Eva Smith 'hadn't been able to save much out of what Birling and Company had paid her' (p. 19) rings true.

ACT TWO: MORE REVELATIONS

- Gerald admits that he met Daisy Renton in the spring of the previous year and that she was his mistress for six months.
- Sheila is hurt and angry at Gerald's involvement with the girl, yet she feels a certain respect for the openness of his admission.
- Mrs Birling tries to bully the Inspector and to control events.
- Sheila realises that the Inspector's enquiries are well founded, and that her mother might also have had some dealings with the girl.
- While Eric is out of the room, Mrs Birling is forced to admit that the girl asked for the help of a charity she worked for and was refused.
- It is revealed that the girl was pregnant, and Mrs Birling lays the blame for the girl's death on the father of the unborn child.
- There is a suspicion that Eric might have been the father of that unborn child.

ACT THREE: THE INSPECTOR LEAVES BUT THE MYSTERY CONTINUES

- Eric confesses that he got the girl pregnant and that he stole money from his father's firm to support her.
- Learning that the girl had appealed to his mother for help and been turned down, Eric blames his mother for the girl's death.
- The Inspector makes a dramatic speech about the consequences of the kind of social irresponsibility that Mr Birling was preaching at the end of the dinner.
- The Inspector, having shown that each had a part in ruining the girl's life, leaves.
- Between them Gerald and Mr Birling gradually prove that the man was not a real police inspector.
- A telephone call to the Chief Constable establishes that there is no Inspector Goole on the police force.
- A telephone call to the Infirmary reveals that there has been no recent suicide.
- Eric and Sheila continue to feel guilty about what they have done, but the others now shrug off any guilt.
- Mr Birling answers the telephone: a young woman has just died on her way to the Infirmary and an inspector is on his way to make enquiries.

TOP TIP (A01)

When writing about a specific scene or extract, try to make connections with the play as a whole, where relevant. For example, when discussing the Inspector you could note that there is a change in the stage directions so the light becomes 'brighter and harder' (p. 1). The harsher light tells us that the Inspector is an important figure who is about to bring a harsh reality into the lives of the Birlings and Gerald Croft, and also suggests that he may affect the course of events.

REVISION FOCUS: CHARACTER TIMELINE

On a timeline, plot each character's involvement in the life of Eva Smith as it is revealed. Make sure you list the events in chronological order. Include the Inspector's involvement too, so that you begin your timeline with his arrival at the Birling house. Note the Act and page in which each event occurs.

ACT ONE, PART 1: CELEBRATING THE ENGAGEMENT (pp. 1–7)

SUMMARY

- The Birlings and Gerald Croft are enjoying a dinner to celebrate the engagement of Gerald to Sheila.
- Sheila, partly serious and partly light-hearted, reproaches Gerald for neglecting her last summer. Mrs Birling, who says little, stresses that men like Gerald and Mr Birling are committed to their businesses.
- Eric, who is slightly drunk, suddenly bursts out laughing, to the annoyance of his parents and Sheila.
- Mr Birling makes a speech congratulating the engaged couple and expressing his pleasure at the match. He hopes their marriage will lead to closer links and greater profits for the Birling and Croft companies.
- The family raise a toast to the couple and, to Sheila's delight, Gerald presents her with an engagement ring.
- Mr Birling gives another speech dismissing recent strikes among the workers and extolling his belief in a successful future for employers like himself. He also dismisses the possibility of a war with Germany.
- Mrs Birling, Sheila and Eric exit, leaving Mr Birling and Gerald to enjoy port and cigars.

WHY IS THIS SECTION IMPORTANT?

A It introduces five of the main **characters** and establishes the **relationships** between them.

B It demonstrates the **wealth** and **social position** of the Birling and Croft families.

C It hints at Mr Birling's **attitudes** to life, marriage, money and business.

D It introduces key ideas about **social justice**, the divisions between the social classes and how life will develop in the future.

KEY CHARACTERS: THE BIRLINGS AND GERALD

J. B. Priestley presents all the main characters in this opening scene. Mr Birling is the head of the family, a man of business, who likes to make pompous speeches. He is delighted at the engagement between Sheila and Gerald, since it will expand his business. However, his lack of concern about relationships between employers and the work force, and about the possibility of war, suggest that his judgement is poor. Mrs Birling is reserved, says little and places great importance on correct behaviour. Eric finds self-control difficult. He drinks too much and is ill at ease in company. By contrast, Sheila is confident and happy to be engaged to Gerald, a sociable, polite, upper-class man of thirty, who seems fond of Sheila. Nonetheless, Priestley raises doubts in the audience's mind about how honest and loving the relationship between the couple really is when Sheila playfully questions Gerald about his neglect of her the previous summer.

TOP TIP: WRITING ABOUT GERALD'S MOTIVES (A01)

When Mrs Birling defends Gerald's neglect of Sheila, she comments that 'men with important work to do ... have to spend ... their time and energy on their business' (p. 3). This hints that Mrs Birling is used to her husband neglecting their marriage and also reinforces the idea that there was a reason Gerald neglected Sheila – one that might have a bearing on the development of the play.

EXAM FOCUS: WRITING ABOUT MR BIRLING (A03)

Read what one student has written about Mr Birling's character and attitudes.

> Priestley uses the character of Mr Birling to show how out of touch the wealthy could be before the First World War. Mr Birling's confidence that prosperity will continue, that trouble with the work force, is 'a lot of wild talk' and that war is highly unlikely creates the effect that he is unable to understand what is happening in the world around him. Not only did strikes increase, but also the First World War was to begin two years later. In addition, Mr Birling sees technology as only linked to progress so that his remarks about the Titanic as 'unsinkable' are ironic as well as bad judgement.

A good example of what Mr Birling represents

A useful connective to highlight an extra point

A clear example of a literary technique (irony) used by Priestley to create effects

Now you try it:

Add a sentence to say how Mr Birling imagines 1940 and why this was ironic for the British audience watching the first performance of the play in 1946.

KEY SETTING: THE DINING ROOM (A03)

In his stage directions, J. B. Priestley describes how the set should look, so the family's privileged lifestyle is clear. The dining room has 'good solid furniture' (p. 1). The champagne, port and cigars all reflect a very comfortable lifestyle where luxury is taken for granted. The hard furniture also suggests a lack of family warmth, despite the luxury, and the formal nature of the dinner party suggests the family's wealth.

KEY CONTEXT: WEALTH AND BUSINESS (A03)

Priestley is preparing us for the contrast we will see between the lifestyle of the wealthy and the hardships endured by those they employ. The references to business and to the Croft family's higher social standing and greater wealth indicate the things Mr Birling values. Although he comes from a modest background, he sees Sheila's marriage to Gerald as the beginning of a powerful business empire.

CHECKPOINT 1 (A01)

Mr Birling has distinct views. How would you describe his character so far?

ACT ONE, PART 2: A CONFIDENTIAL CHAT (pp. 8–11)

SUMMARY

- Mr Birling and Gerald Croft remain in the dining room where Mr Birling wonders if Lady Croft is concerned that Sheila is of a lower social class than Gerald.
- Gerald politely dismisses Mr Birling's worries. Mr Birling mentions that he is likely to get a knighthood in the New Year's Honours List and is pleased when Gerald suggests that he drop a hint to his mother.
- Gerald and Mr Birling joke about a scandal ruining that possibility.
- Eric returns, pours himself a drink, and tells them the women are talking about clothes, so there is no hurry.
- Mr Birling claims that to women clothes are a mark of self-respect. Eric, about to recall something, stops himself abruptly.
- They are interrupted by someone at the front door. It is a police inspector and Mr Birling, who is a magistrate, assumes he has come for a warrant.
- Gerald jokes that Eric may have been 'up to something' (p. 10). Eric is not amused.

WHY IS THIS SECTION IMPORTANT?

A   It allows Mr Birling to **talk** with Gerald while the rest of the family are **not present**.

B   It reveals the **selfish** way in which the Birlings and Crofts think.

C   We learn that Mr Birling, despite his wealth, feels **socially inferior** to the Crofts.

D   It is revealed that Mr Birling is in line for a **knighthood**.

E   There are **hints** about **secrets** that could affect the **characters** in the future.

KEY THEME: STATUS AND AMBITION

In this section Priestley shows us how ambitious Mr Birling is to gain social status, and how much he believes in each man for himself and his own. Mr Birling fears that Lady Croft may not wholly approve of Sheila because the Birlings are of a lower social class and, since Lord and Lady Croft are absent from the engagement dinner, there is a hint that Mr Birling's fears may be justified. Nonetheless, we suspect that the Birling's wealth is sufficiently attractive to the Crofts for them to agree to the marriage. We see another example of Mr Birling's ambition when he tells Gerald (and, via him, Lady Croft) that he expects a knighthood. However, his most important characteristic is his belief that a man has no responsibilities to the wider community. Inspector Goole will challenge this view, and responsibility to others will be a constant theme throughout the play.

KEY QUOTATION: DRAMATIC DEVICES (A02)

Gerald's comment to Mr Birling, 'You seem to be a nice well-behaved family' (p. 8) would alert a perceptive audience to the possibility that the Birlings are no such thing, and it would be Priestley's intention to create this effect. Dramatic irony of this kind is one of the most common devices used in the play.

TOP TIP (A02)

Make a list of all the quotations between pages 8 and 11, up to the Inspector's entrance, that hint at revelations to come as the play progresses.

AIMING HIGH: COMMENT ON LINKS TO THEMES ★

Mr Birling's joke that he expects a knighthood, provided that the Birlings don't 'start a scandal' (p. 8), and Gerald's joke that Eric may have been up to something 'fishy' (p. 9) alert the audience to the likelihood of a scandal. These comments illustrate Priestley's use of irony and also link to the wider themes of the play, such as hypocrisy and responsibility. For example, Mr Birling is happy to accept a knighthood from the community while he dismisses his responsibility to the community, revealing his hypocrisy. Eric's irresponsibility and lack of concern for others results in Eva Smith's pregnancy (p. 53). You will gain more marks if you mention these links to the wider themes of the play.

You can also show how Mrs Birling's and Sheila's preoccupation with clothes (p. 9) links to Eva Smith's story and the theme of responsibility. A dress is at the centre of Eva Smith's sacking from Milwards – a dress that suits Eva Smith better than Sheila, who is jealous, and Sheila is responsible for Eva Smith's dismissal (pp. 20–2).

ACT ONE, PART 3: AN INSPECTOR INTERRUPTS (pp. 11–16)

SUMMARY

- An Inspector enters the room. Mr Birling tries to take control of the situation. He mentions his standing in the community, but the Inspector is unimpressed.
- The Inspector has come to make enquiries about the suicide of a girl who has died after drinking disinfectant.
- Eric is shocked. Mr Birling is more interested in why the Inspector is visiting. The Inspector says that there was a letter and a diary in the girl's room. She had more than one name, including Eva Smith.
- The Inspector shows Mr Birling a photograph of Eva Smith, but refuses to show Gerald or Eric.
- Mr Birling recognises the girl. He claims her suicide had nothing to do with her dismissal two years previously as a ringleader of a strike.
- Eric objects to his father's actions. Mr Birling justifies them and Gerald supports him. In an attempt to silence the Inspector, Mr Birling says the Chief Constable is his friend.
- Eric and Mr Birling continue to argue about Mr Birling's sacking of Eva Smith. Mr Birling sees no need for the Inspector to question him further. Sheila enters.

WHY IS THIS SECTION IMPORTANT?

A The celebratory **atmosphere** is interrupted by the arrival of the Inspector, who has a commanding presence.
B We see Mr Birling **losing control** of events.
C A **link** is made between the **suicide** of Eva Smith and the Birlings.
D Eric **opposes** his father's decision to sack Eva Smith.

KEY CHARACTERS: MR BIRLING AND THE INSPECTOR (A02)

Priestley presents the Inspector and Mr Birling as opposites. When the Inspector enters, the stage directions tell us he creates 'an impression of massiveness, solidity and purposefulness' (p. 11). Priestley is telling us that the Inspector will almost certainly have an impact on future events, and from the outset the Inspector takes command of the situation. He 'has a disconcerting habit of looking hard' (p. 11) at someone before speaking, he takes his time and interrupts Mr Birling, 'cutting through' (p. 12) his bluster. Mr Birling, by contrast, adopts a condescending manner towards the Inspector and shows increasing 'impatience' (p. 11). Finally he resorts to bullying when he realises that the Inspector will do his 'duty' (p. 15) and not be diverted. The biggest difference between the two is the Inspector's determination to pursue justice for Eva Smith, and Mr Birling's determination to 'keep labour costs down' (p. 15) at the expense of his work force.

KEY QUOTATION: ASKING FOR THE EARTH A02

When the Inspector says, 'But after all it's better to ask for the earth than to take it' (p. 15), he is replying to Mr Birling's justification for sacking Eva Smith. The Inspector's comment links closely to his monologue in the final act (p. 56), in which he warns the Birlings and Gerald of potential conflict to come if his message of responsibility to others is ignored.

TOP TIP A02

Note how the Inspector's arrival interrupts Mr Birling expressing his disregard for community responsibility. This is ironic when we learn that the Inspector has arrived to try to teach them about what responsibility really means.

KEY STRUCTURE: THE CHAIN BEGINS A02

Priestley uses the Inspector to outline the idea of a 'chain of events' (p. 14) leading to Eva Smith's death. Although Eva Smith was a good worker, Mr Birling's refusal to take her back after the strike means that he is the first link in the chain. When he asks the Inspector 'what happened to her after that?' (p. 16) he unwittingly invites the Inspector to reveal the next link in the chain.

EXAM FOCUS: WRITING ABOUT EVA SMITH A01

You may be asked to write about important features of the play. Here is what one student has written about the way Priestley presents the character of Eva Smith:

> The Inspector introduces the character of Eva Smith. He has her letter 'and a sort of diary' and is able to outline a chain of events leading to her death. However, we never meet her and only see her through the Inspector's eyes, and the other characters who assume she is the same person that each of them knew. Mr Birling seems cruel and unsympathetic towards her. The Inspector, a good man, shows sympathy and consequently we assume that Priestley shares his view. Eva Smith's life is at the centre of the play because...

Connective adverb helps develop a related point

A key point about Eva Smith's story

Conjunctive adverb connects clauses showing cause and effect

Now you try it:

Finish the final sentence saying who or what Eva Smith represents in society and what Priestley means by creating her.

ACT ONE, PART 4: SHEILA'S LINK IN THE CHAIN (pp. 16–21)

SUMMARY

- Sheila returns. Mr Birling assumes the Inspector will now leave and is annoyed when he wants to question Sheila.
- Sheila is shocked by the description of the girl's suicide and Mr Birling becomes less aggressive when he realises that the Inspector wants to question others in the family who might know something of the girl's life.
- Sheila, Eric and Gerald claim no knowledge of Eva Smith and the Inspector reminds them that she used more than one name.
- The Inspector describes Eva Smith's struggle to find work after her dismissal from Birlings, explaining that there are many young women like Eva Smith. He says she was very lucky to get a job in the dress shop, Milwards.
- On hearing that Eva Smith was sacked from Milwards because a customer complained about her, Sheila becomes agitated. The Inspector shows her a photograph.
- Sheila runs from the room crying.

WHY IS THIS SECTION IMPORTANT?

A   Both Eric and Sheila feel sympathy for Eva Smith.

B   Sheila is horrified by the story of Eva Smith's death.

C   Mr Birling senses a possible scandal as Eva Smith's story takes on greater significance for the family.

D   We realise there is a new link in the chain since Sheila recognises Eva Smith.

KEY THEME: COMMUNITY RESPONSIBILITY

In this section Priestley shows us the divide that is emerging between Mr Birling and his children with regard to the main **theme** of the play: our responsibility to others and the idea of community. Mr Birling's treatment of Eva Smith is frowned on by Sheila, who protests, 'But these girls aren't cheap labour – they're *people*' (p. 19). Eric agrees, but Mr Birling is far more self-interested. His main concern in this section is to quash any hint of scandal, so that no doubts should threaten his knighthood and his respectability. These take priority over any sense of duty to his work force and women such as Eva Smith.

KEY CONTEXT

Before the First World War many working women in the United Kingdom worked as domestic servants. As a factory or shop worker, Eva Smith might have expected to have more freedom. So she would have felt more confident about going on strike.

KEY CHARACTERS: SHEILA AND EVA (A02)

Both women are of similar age, but while Sheila is celebrating her engagement, Eva Smith is dead and lying in the hospital mortuary. Sheila has an affluent life, while Eva lived in poverty, 'lonely' and 'half-starved' (p. 19). These contrasts emphasise Eva's unhappiness and Priestley always presents her in a sympathetic light, for example, through the Inspector's description of her as 'very pretty' (p. 18). Consequently, when Sheila sees the photograph and the audience realises that she was the customer who 'complained' (p. 20), causing the girl's dismissal from Milwards, the effect is to create dramatic tension. We see that Sheila is, indeed, the next link in the chain and we wait for the details to unfold.

KEY QUOTATION: SHEILA'S ALARM (A01)

Sheila's comment, 'What do you mean by saying that? You talk as if we were responsible' (p. 18) is ironic because the audience suspects that the Birlings and Gerald do bear some responsibility for Eva Smith's death. Through these words of Sheila's, Priestley alerts the audience to the possibility of the characters' involvement.

AIMING HIGH: COMMENT ON THE PHOTOGRAPH AS A DEVICE ⭐

Another example of how Priestley creates dramatic tension is the use of the photograph as a device. The Inspector controls who sees the photograph and when, and it has an instant effect on the character viewing it. Sheila, for example, recognises Eva Smith and gives 'a little cry, ... a half-stifled sob' (p. 21) that raises or confirms suspicions in the audience. Importantly, no single character can ever be sure that they have seen the same photograph as another. This helps the Inspector to control the plot as well as the characters.

However, you will show a fuller understanding if you also consider whether Priestley's use of this device is well handled. For example, is the way the Inspector controls who sees the photograph believable? Would a police inspector behave in this way? Does the device make the plot seem clumsy? Or is the Inspector so different from the usual police inspector that we accept his behaviour as part of his mysterious presence? Be sure you have reasons for the view you choose and support what you say by referring to the play.

CHECKPOINT 3 (A01)

What do we learn from the Inspector about Eva Smith in Act One?

KEY CONTEXT (A03)

An Inspector Calls is sometimes referred to as a 'well-made play'. This idea arose in the nineteenth century and refers to the way a play is carefully constructed, such as through Priestley's use of the photograph to create twists and turns in the plot.

ACT ONE, PART 5: SHEILA'S CONFESSION (pp. 21–6)

SUMMARY

- Eric realises that Sheila knows who Eva Smith is. Mr Birling is angry with the Inspector for upsetting Sheila and goes out to tell his wife what is happening.
- Inspector Goole remains unperturbed. He refuses to show Gerald the photograph or to let Eric leave.
- Sheila returns. She feels guilty that she was the cause of Eva Smith's dismissal, but the Inspector shows no sympathy for Sheila.
- Sheila explains that she requested Eva Smith's sacking from Milwards because the dress Sheila liked suited Eva Smith better and this made Sheila cross. Eric is surprised by Sheila's actions.
- The Inspector makes Sheila understand that her jealousy contributed to Eva's downfall. He adds that Eva Smith changed her name to Daisy Renton and Gerald reacts sharply. Sheila is immediately alerted. The Inspector leaves the room with Eric.
- Sheila warns Gerald not to try to hide the truth and he does not deny the affair he had with Daisy Renton/Eva Smith, but suggests they say nothing to the Inspector. Sheila laughs, knowing full well that the Inspector already knows.

TOP TIP

List examples from Act One, with quotations, that show the similarities and differences between Sheila Birling and Eva Smith's circumstances, appearance and natures. Keep it as a reference.

WHY IS THIS SECTION IMPORTANT?

A We see Mr Birling's desire to **protect** his daughter.

B Sheila's **link in the chain** of events becomes clear.

C The Inspector's position is becoming more **powerful** and he reveals more information about Eva Smith.

D We see how people can **misuse wealth** and **social status**.

E Sheila and Gerald's **relationship** becomes strained and we realise Gerald is the **next link in the chain**.

KEY THEME: GUILT (A02)

Priestley reveals the power that privilege and wealth have by showing how Sheila, as the 'daughter of a good customer' (p. 24) at Milwards ensured that Eva Smith was sacked. Sheila's assumption that Eva would manage subsequently, shows her naivety about the way people like Eva live, and her realisation that she was a catalyst in Eva's decline create feelings of intense guilt. The Inspector points out that Sheila's remorse comes 'too late' for Eva Smith. (p. 24). However, this is the beginning of Sheila's development as a character. Gradually, through the Inspector's words she is becoming more aware of the world beyond her narrow experience.

KEY FORM: AN EXIT, A SECRET, A CLIMAX (A02)

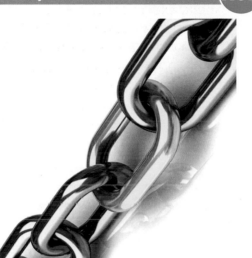

After Gerald's 'startled' (p. 25) response to the name Daisy Renton, the Inspector exits with Eric. Sheila can now confront Gerald about his secret affair. Tension is raised. Sheila calls Gerald 'a fool' (p. 26) for his vain suggestion that the Inspector need never be told about the affair, and the climax is reached when she dramatically declares that the Inspector already knows. As the curtain falls, the audience sees that Gerald is the next link in the chain.

KEY LANGUAGE: REPETITION (A02)

Repetition is a device Priestley uses to give power to a character's voice. Mr Birling complains that the Inspector, by upsetting Sheila, has made 'a nasty mess' (p. 21) of the celebratory dinner. The Inspector repeats these words and applies them to Eva Smith's life, 'a nasty mess somebody's made of it' (p. 21). The Inspector's scornful reply reveals the trivial nature of Mr Birling's concerns compared with Eva Smith's death, and also the Inspector's self-assurance and growing control over the characters. His voice will reach its most rhetorical in his final speech, where he uses much repetition (p. 56).

REVISION FOCUS: THE INSPECTOR'S WORDS

- Reread the Inspector's speech about the 'dead girl' (p. 25).
- Create a two-column table. Head the first 'Reason' and the second 'Evidence'.
- Under the first column, write down four reasons why Priestley creates this speech.
- In the second column, support your reasons with evidence (such as quotations or references).

ACT TWO, PART 1: GUILTY FEELINGS (pp. 27–9)

SUMMARY

- The Inspector enters. Gerald encourages Sheila to leave but, although the Inspector allows her to go, she prefers to hear the details of Gerald's affair with Daisy Renton.
- Gerald resents Sheila's decision to stay and hear the details of his affair with Daisy Renton. He thinks Sheila wishes to see his discomfort when he is questioned.
- Sheila challenges Gerald's doubts about her and believes Gerald does not love her because of her treatment of Eva Smith.
- The Inspector intervenes. He points out that Sheila wishes to stay because she does not want to shoulder all the blame for Eva Smith's death, nor should she.
- The Inspector emphasises that they have to share the guilt.
- Mrs Birling enters.

KEY CONTEXT (A03)

It was not uncommon for upper-class and wealthy middle-class Edwardian men to have mistresses or to meet women (as Gerald, Eric and Alderman Meggarty do) providing it did not become public and there was no scandal.

WHY IS THIS SECTION IMPORTANT?

A Sheila and Gerald's quarrel reveals a **lack of trust** and **understanding** in their **relationship**.

B The Inspector emphasises **shared responsibility** to others and has a growing influence on Sheila.

C While Sheila's sense of **guilt** does not lessen, she believes she is not the only one to blame.

KEY THEME: SHEILA AND GERALD – TRUE LOVE? (A01)

Priestley reveals that Sheila and Gerald's relationship is not an honest one. The revelations that occurred in Act One about Sheila's dealings with Eva Smith and Gerald's affair with her (as Daisy Renton) have already put a strain on Sheila and Gerald's relationship and they begin to grow suspicious of each other. When Gerald suggests that Sheila should leave the dining room because she has had a 'long, exciting and tiring day' (p. 27) and Sheila refuses, he suspects her motives.

Sheila's shock that Gerald can think so badly of her, reveals he does not understand her. She in turn assumes he must see her as 'a selfish, vindictive creature' (p. 28) for her treatment of Eva Smith. All these doubts suggest that neither knows the other sufficiently well and that the relationship is not founded on trust and sympathy. Part of the Inspector's role is to peel away the self-assured layers of the Birlings' and Gerald's lives to reveal what lies underneath, and Sheila and Gerald's relationship is becoming a casualty.

KEY QUOTATION: ATTITUDES TO WOMEN (A01)

The Inspector's comment, 'And you think young women ought to be protected against unpleasant and disturbing things?' (p. 27) and Gerald's reply that he does, display different attitudes to middle-class Edwardian women. Aside from Gerald not wanting Sheila to hear about his affair, he adopts the Edwardian view that women are not to be tainted by unpleasant, worldly truths, or are not capable of dealing with them. The Inspector holds a more modern view and also points to class hypocrisy in the treatment of Eva Smith: while middle-class women are to be protected from the harsh realities of life, poorer, working-class women are not.

KEY CHARACTER: SHEILA'S GROWING AWARENESS (A02)

The Inspector's bluntness and unsparing criticism of Sheila's behaviour does not make her dislike or disapprove of him. On the contrary, she is drawn to him and stares at him, 'wonderingly' (p. 29). His mysterious presence affects her and she finds that she agrees with his view. The audience is witnessing how the Inspector is influencing the young.

AIMING HIGH: COMMENT ON THE INSPECTOR'S ROLE

Priestley creates a moral figure in the Inspector to drive home to the audience how much Eva Smith suffered and to elicit the audience's sympathy and condemnation of those who have mistreated her. However, the Inspector also knows that Sheila alone is not to blame. When he says, 'we'll have to share our guilt,' (p. 29) he is referring to both a shared responsibility for Eva Smith's death and to our collective responsibility for others like Eva Smith. The full weight of his moral position, that we are all responsible for each other, will gather impact as the play develops.

However, to present a fuller understanding of this position you could discuss Priestley's beliefs, *embodied in the Inspector,* which are tied to a moral socialism (as opposed to Mr Birling's individualism that focuses on himself). This is a political belief that says there is a need for cooperation, community and social justice in society. The play is a vehicle for Priestley's views and an attempt to influence the 1946 audience only just free of war and ready to build a new society.

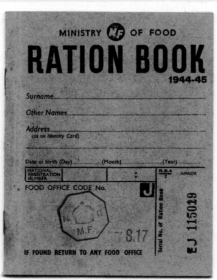

TOP TIP (A01)

Find quotations in this section that sum up Sheila's attitude to Gerald. For example what does this tell you about her feelings towards him when she says: 'Yes, but you don't believe me. And this is just the wrong time not to believe me' (p. 28).

TOP TIP (A01)

It is important to understand why the Inspector intervenes in the quarrel between Sheila and Gerald. Reread his dialogue on p. 29 and underline key words. For example, 'understand'.

ACT TWO, PART 2: ENTER MRS BIRLING (pp. 29–32)

SUMMARY

- Mrs Birling enters, unaware of what has been happening between Sheila and Gerald, and introduces herself to the Inspector. Sheila objects to her mother's over-confidence.
- Mrs Birling thinks that Sheila's interest in Eva Smith's death is an unhealthy curiosity and she encourages her to leave the dining room.
- Sheila tries to warn her mother that the Inspector can break down any defences, but Mrs Birling does not understand.
- When the Inspector takes Sheila's part, Mrs Birling tries to impress the Inspector by reminding him of her husband's importance in the community.
- Gerald cuts in to advise Mrs Birling not to persist in trying to impress the Inspector.
- Mrs Birling explains that Mr Birling and Eric will be coming back soon and that Eric, untypically, is a little drunk. She is shocked to find from Sheila that Eric regularly drinks too much. Gerald confirms what Sheila has said.
- Mrs Birling accuses Sheila of being the one who is destroying the family's reputation.

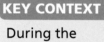

KEY CONTEXT **A03**

During the Edwardian period, a Police Inspector such as Inspector Goole would be regarded as lower middle class. Mrs Birling would see herself very much as a social superior. A Chief Inspector, such as Mr Birling's friend Colonel Roberts, would be seen as thoroughly middle class.

WHY IS THIS SECTION IMPORTANT?

A Priestley draws a sharp **contrast** between Mrs Birling and Sheila.

B Mrs Birling's attempts to use **her position** to bully the Inspector fail.

C Mrs Birling's **ignorance** of Eric's drinking show us she is **insensitive and** out of touch with her son.

D Sheila recognises the Inspector's ability to break down defences and **control** situations.

KEY CHARACTERS: MRS BIRLING AND SHEILA **A02**

Sheila's growing awareness of the Inspector's viewpoint and her concern for her family's part in Eva Smith's downfall starkly contrasts with Mrs Birling's understanding of what is happening. Mrs Birling enters the dining room *'briskly and self-confidently, quite out of key'* (p. 29) with the atmosphere. While she is unaware of the conversation that has just taken place between Sheila, Gerald and the Inspector, she is also unable to sense the mood in the room, suggesting she lacks awareness of other people. Sheila's attempt to warn her mother that she is *'beginning all wrong'* (p. 29) is fruitless. Mrs Birling does not grasp what Sheila means when she says, *'you mustn't try to build a kind of wall between us and that girl'* (p. 30) because the welfare of her husband's employees are of no concern to her.

When the Inspector agrees with Sheila, Mrs Birling takes offence because he does not pay due regard to her position and rank. For Mrs Birling, social position matters. The Inspector holds no fascination for her, as he does for her daughter. She sees him as a social inferior, who is a threat to her well-ordered life. Consequently, she tries to threaten him by reminding him (just as Mr Birling did) of her husband's position as 'Lord Mayor only two years ago' (p. 31). If we consider that Sheila and her mother were light-heartedly 'talking about clothes' (p. 9) earlier in the evening we can see how a rift between them is growing.

TOP TIP (A01)

Note how Priestley presents the Inspector in this section. What mood does the Inspector adopt? How does he manage Mrs Birling? How does he control the situation?

KEY QUOTATION: IMPRESSING THE YOUNG (A01)

The Inspector's comment, 'We often do [make an impression] on the young ones. They're more impressionable' (p. 30) is said in answer to Mrs Birling's haughty observation that he has made an impression on Sheila. Priestley is suggesting that the young are more open minded than the older generation about the kind of society they want to live in, in this case one in which people care and feel responsible for the wider community. We have already seen how Sheila is influenced by the Inspector's words and mystified by him (p. 29). Eric showed earlier (p. 15) that he does not agree with his father's attitude to his work force.

EXAM FOCUS: WRITING ABOUT ERIC'S PROBLEMS (A01)

Here is what one student has written about the way Priestley presents Mrs Birling's understanding of Eric:

> Priestley indicates how little Mrs Birling knows about her son through her ignorance of his drinking. She excuses him to the Inspector by saying that Eric has had 'rather too much to drink tonight'. Sheila immediately tells her mother the truth in an attempt to 'stop these silly pretences' because she is aware that the Inspector is concerned about truth and Mrs Birling is not facing the truth. When Gerald supports Sheila, Mrs Birling's responds 'bitterly' complaining about the unsuitability of the occasion to give her the news.

A strong opening line

A quotation embedded successfully in the sentence

Key point about the Inspector

Now you try it:

Add a final sentence saying what Mrs Birling's response tells us about her relationship with Eric.

ACT TWO, PART 3: GERALD'S REVELATIONS (pp. 32–40)

SUMMARY

- Mr Birling has been trying unsuccessfully to persuade Eric to go to bed.
- Mr Birling is annoyed by the Inspector's insistence that he question Eric, and in his own time.
- Sheila protests that her father's high-handed approach to the Inspector is pointless. Mrs Birling dismisses Sheila's protests as 'over-excitement' (p. 33).
- The Inspector confronts Gerald and asks how he knew Daisy Renton. Mr and Mrs Birling are shocked.
- Gerald's tries to deny that he knew Daisy Renton and then admits he met her the previous year in the bar at the Palace Theatre. He asks Sheila to leave. Sheila refuses.
- Gerald explains that he rescued Daisy Renton from the clutches of Alderman Meggarty. She later became Gerald's mistress when he rented rooms and provided her with money. Sheila is resentful and sarcastic towards Gerald. Gerald says he is uncertain whether he loved Daisy Renton and that he ended the affair in the September.
- The Inspector explains that Daisy Renton left for the seaside where she stayed for two months to be alone and to think. Gerald expresses his sadness. Sheila thanks Gerald for being honest, but returns the engagement ring.

WHY IS THIS SECTION IMPORTANT?

A   The Inspector exerts increasingly greater **control** over the situation.

B   Gerald reveals his affair through the **Inspector's questioning** and we see both Gerald and the girl in a **different way**.

C   Sheila **breaks off** her engagement to Gerald but leaves the way open for a **fresh** look at their **relationship**.

KEY LANGUAGE: EUPHEMISM

Priestley uses **euphemism** such as 'women of the town' (p. 34) in this section of the play. It is in keeping with the characters since they would use a less blunt way of referring to prostitution. Note how Sheila sarcastically repeats 'women of the town' when she asks Gerald to continue with his story. Reference to prostitution, even euphemistically, would not usually occur in middle-class circles in front of women, but in the play Inspector Goole is forcing the Birlings and Gerald to face the realities of Daisy Renton's life.

TOP TIP **A01**

Follow Gerald's relationship with Daisy Renton noting when it started and ended, its duration and where it took place.

CHECKPOINT 5 **A01**

Earlier, Mr Birling refused to accept any blame for Eva Smith's death. How does Gerald's confession contrast with Mr Birling's attitude?

KEY CONTEXT: EDWARDIAN RESPECTABILITY (A03)

Whatever Gerald's feelings for Daisy Renton and Sheila, which may be genuine, it is not simply a matter of whom he loved best. His affair, if known, would cause a scandal. Daisy Renton, though 'fresh and charming' (p. 35) was poor, working class and 'a woman of the town' (p. 34) and 'being found out' was as much a social crime as having a mistress. This is exemplified in Mrs Birling's refusal to hear about 'this disgusting affair' (p. 38). The Inspector's questioning exposes this kind of hypocrisy. For Gerald and Sheila's relationship to continue they would need to confront these double standards and get 'to know each other' (p. 40) honestly.

KEY QUOTATION: THE INSPECTOR'S POWER (A02)

The Inspector's comment, 'As soon as I mentioned the name Daisy Renton, it was obvious you'd known her' (p. 33), not only reinforces Sheila's comment (p. 25) recognising the same thing, it is another signal to the audience that Gerald's relationship will be revealed. Priestley, through the Inspector, is introducing the next link in the chain of events as well as highlighting the Inspector's increasing control of the situation.

TOP TIP (A02)

Remember that Priestley uses the diary as a device to explain how the Inspector knows so much about the events of Daisy Renton's/Eva Smith's life. His knowledge also adds to his power over the other characters. Make a note of where the Inspector refers to the diary in this section and in Act One and how he uses it.

EXAM FOCUS: WRITING ABOUT DAISY RENTON (A02)

Here is what one student has written about Daisy Renton's situation after her affair with Gerald is over:

> Priestley is careful to portray Daisy Renton in a quiet, thoughtful mood when the Inspector tell us that she went to the seaside to 'remember' the good times with Gerald. The effect is to make the audience especially sympathetic towards her. The Inspector's account of her upsets Gerald. We see his compassionate side and he regrets the hurt he caused. Priestley also shows us that this was her happiest time, making the audience feel that if her relationship with Gerald, which had no future, was the best there was then she must have felt she had no future. Most importantly, her feelings of sadness are the first signs of the depression that will lead to her death and ...

Shows a feature of Gerald's character

Adverb phrase draws attention to a key idea

Sound reference to the effects Priestley creates

Now you try it:

Finish the sentence, commenting on Gerald's link in Daisy Renton's story.

ACT TWO, PART 5: MRS BIRLING'S IDEA OF CHARITY (pp. 42–9)

SUMMARY

- The Inspector questions Mrs Birling about the Brumley Women's Charity Organization, which helps women in trouble.
- Mrs Birling says they give help to those who deserve it. She was chairing the meeting two weeks ago.
- Mr Birling returns. Eric is not in his room. The Inspector says Eric is needed, but refuses to say more.
- The committee interviewed a girl (under the name of Mrs Birling) two weeks earlier. Mrs Birling regarded the use of her name as insolent and felt justified in using her influence to refuse help.
- The Inspector insists that Mrs Birling was wrong because Eva Smith was pregnant.
- Mrs Birling says the father of the unborn child should be held responsible. Sheila is horrified by her mother's attitude and Mr Birling is worried that his wife's actions will cause a scandal.
- Mrs Birling refused to believe the girl's account that the father was young and irresponsible and that she had rejected his stolen money.
- Mrs Birling says the father should be held entirely to blame if the story is true and Sheila begs her mother to stop. Eric enters.

WHY IS THIS SECTION IMPORTANT?

A Mrs Birling's **link** to Eva Smith is established.

B We see the characters' **different reactions** to events.

C We see the Inspector as **prosecutor** and **judge**.

D Eva Smith's **pregnancy** is revealed.

E Mrs Birling's insistence that the father of the unborn child is to **blame** for the girl's **death** leads to the **dramatic** ending of the Act.

KEY CONTEXT (A03)

Most Edwardians would regard Eva Smith as 'a fallen woman'; an unmarried woman who had lost her virginity. When Mrs Birling holds the young man 'entirely responsible' (p. 48) she reflects the attitude that a woman's place was under the authority of a man, whether it was a husband, father or another man. Much of society did not regard women as independent citizens.

AIMING HIGH: CLASS PREJUDICE

Priestley depicts class prejudice through several characters, in particular Mrs Birling. She has a clear-cut code in which families like hers and the Crofts are near the top of the social pile and young women like Eva Smith are

squarely at the bottom. Due to this class prejudice, Mrs Birling cannot believe that Eva Smith, or 'a girl in her position', could have 'fine feelings and scruples' (p. 46) and would refuse Eric's stolen money. Mr Birling and Gerald's exchange about the irresponsibility of the workers managing their money (p. 15) shows a similar attitude to class. Eric visits the Palace bar not only to drink, but also to seek women from the lower class.

However, to gain higher marks you should show how class prejudice is evident in the Birling character we are sympathetic to: Sheila. Her display of anger at Milwards, because she felt that Eva Smith had been 'very impertinent' (p. 24), echoes Mr Birling's attitude. Her prejudice springs not only from jealousy of Eva Smith's looks, but because the lower-class Eva Smith is not respectful enough of Sheila's higher status. The effect is that each of the Birlings and Gerald in their different ways displayed the kind of class prejudice that shaped Eva Smith's life.

KEY STRUCTURE: DRAMATIC EFFECT

Priestley carefully builds the tension throughout this section and the final effect is highly dramatic. Before the Inspector questions Mrs Birling (p. 42), certain key features are in place. Gerald has not seen Daisy Renton since 'the first week of September' (p. 38) and Eric is absent from the stage. As the questioning continues it turns out that Mrs Birling had interviewed the girl (as 'Mrs Birling') at the charity committee only 'two weeks ago' (p. 43). Eric, when last seen, was 'excitable' (p. 42) and the Inspector wishes to question him. The audience can guess that Eric is likely to be a link in the chain of events.

As the Inspector's interrogation of Mrs Birling progresses it is Sheila who sees what is about to happen. Despite her 'sudden alarm' (p. 48) and her warnings, her mother ignores Sheila's plea to stop demanding that the Inspector does his 'duty' (p. 48) and seek out the father of Eva Smith's unborn child. An important pause in the drama then follows in which the Inspector calmly repeats Mrs Birling's words that he will do his 'duty' (p. 48). The irony is not lost on Mrs Birling as Act Two dramatically reaches a climax with her sudden realisation that the 'drunken young idler' (p. 47) is Eric. At this point Eric enters and the curtain falls.

CHECKPOINT 7

Do you think Eric fits the description of the father of the unborn child and, if so, in what ways?

CHECKPOINT 8

How do Mrs Birling's attitude and language affect the way the audience regard her?

TOP TIP

Sheila is greatly troubled by her mother's reaction to Eva Smith. Find evidence in this section to show her horror and make a note of which statement reveals this most.

ACT THREE, PART 1: ERIC'S LINK IN THE CHAIN (pp. 50–2)

SUMMARY

- The family and the Inspector confront Eric, who acknowledges his involvement with the girl/Eva Smith.
- Sheila tells Eric that their mother feels that the father of the child should be held responsible. Mrs Birling pleads ignorance of Eric's involvement.
- Sheila also tells Eric that she has already revealed that he drinks too much. Eric is angry.
- The Inspector takes control, overruling Mr Birling by allowing Eric to have a drink.
- Eric explains that he met the girl the previous November at the Palace bar when he was drunk.
- Eric and the girl went to her lodgings that night, after Eric insisted. They had sex.
- Mr Birling demands that Sheila take her mother to the drawing room and they leave.

WHY IS THIS SECTION IMPORTANT?

A   The **link** is made between Eric and the girl/Eva Smith and we learn of his association with her.

B   Mrs Birling is **distressed**, overcome by Eric's behaviour and the Inspector's persistence.

C   The Inspector **takes over**.

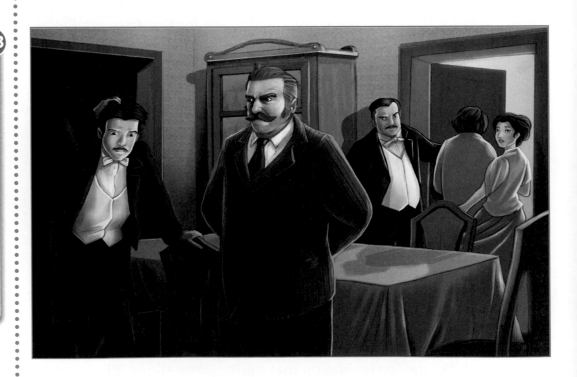

KEY THEME: FAMILY RELATIONSHIPS (A02)

TOP TIP (A02)

Follow how the Inspector talks to the other characters in Act Three by reading the stage directions. Also follow the other characters' responses to him. Keep notes and decide how this shows the Inspector has changed.

As the curtain opens on Act Three, the Birling family and the Inspector are all present *'staring at'* Eric (p. 50). Priestley puts Eric in the spotlight, the last of the Birlings to be held accountable for Eva Smith's death. But Priestley is also showing how the Birling relationships have fractured. The gulf between Eric and his mother is made clear as Mrs Birling protests that 'There must be some mistake' (p. 50). Her inability to accept Eric's involvement with Eva Smith (as well as his drinking, which she denied previously, p. 32), emphasises again how little she knows her son.

When Sheila tells Eric she has already revealed that he drinks too much, 'because it was simply bound to come out' (p. 50), Eric interprets Sheila's honesty as betrayal, calling her a 'little sneak' (p. 50). In response, Mr and Mrs Birling accuse Sheila of disloyalty. When the Inspector grants Eric a whisky he is not only overruling Mr Birling's wishes, he is taking over the father's role, as if Mr Birling is no longer capable. It is the Inspector's comment about adjusting 'family relationships' (p. 51) that gets to the heart of the matter.

EXAM FOCUS: WRITING ABOUT THE INSPECTOR IN CHARGE (A02)

Here is what one student has written about the way Priestley shows how Inspector Goole has taken control of events.

> At the beginning of Act Three, whenever the Inspector speaks it is to question or inform the other characters or tell them what to do. The effect is to make us believe that the Inspector is now in complete charge. One of the most important examples of the Inspector's control is when he counters Mr Birling's 'No' with a 'Yes' when Eric asks for a drink. Mr Birling curbs his temper so that when he follows by saying to Eric, 'All right. Go on.' we can almost feel his resentment. From this point until the Inspector leaves the stage Mr Birling does not challenge him again.

Shows how Priestley creates effects

Precise reference to evidence

Reference to another part of the play develops point

Key point about Mr Birling's reaction

Now you try it:

Add a final sentence saying what you think the Inspector has done to Mr Birling.

ACT THREE, PART 2: ALMOST A FATHER (pp. 52–3)

SUMMARY

- The Inspector questions Eric, who describes how he met the girl/Eva Smith again by accident in the Palace bar.
- Eric learned more about the girl's life. He also reveals his attitude to the women at the Palace bar. He returned to the girl's lodgings.
- Eric and the girl met again, she told him she was pregnant, but did not want to marry him.
- Eric gave her money, about £50, but she refused to accept any more when she discovered it was stolen.
- Eric reveals that he took the money from the Birling office, but denies it was theft. Mr Birling is angry.
- Mrs Birling and Sheila return.

WHY IS THIS SECTION IMPORTANT?

A We learn about **Eric's relationship** with the girl/Eva Smith, her **pregnancy** and why he **stole money**.

B We learn about **Eric's difficulties** admitting the theft.

C The **male** characters speak more **bluntly** without the **female** characters present.

D Eric's involvement with the girl is the **last** to be revealed. He is another **link** in the **chain of events**.

KEY LANGUAGE: A CHOICE OF WORDS (A02)

Once again Priestley gives us an example of how the men behave differently when the women leave the room. For example, in front of his mother Eric avoids saying he had sex with the girl by commenting, 'that's when it happened' (p. 52). While the men still use **euphemism**, the Inspector now feels free to ask if Eric and the girl 'made love' (p. 52). Mr Birling asks if Eric 'had to go to bed with her' (p. 52). Both these phrases would be considered strong language in 1912. This shows us that middle-class women, like Sheila and her mother, are treated as though they were children and we are reminded of the Inspector's earlier comment to Gerald, 'you think young women ought to be protected against unpleasant and disturbing things' (p. 27).

Eric describes the women of the Palace bar as 'fat old tarts' (p. 52), an expression he would never use in his mother's presence. This and Gerald's earlier comment about 'hard-eyed dough-faced women' (p. 34) show the distinction being made between the treatment of middle- and lower-class women. Eric and Gerald's belittling and insulting language show both sexism and class prejudice.

KEY CHARACTER: THE FURTHER DECLINE OF EVA SMITH (A01)

Eva Smith had once been unable to accept the abuse of Alderman Meggarty, but now accepts Eric's drunken approach. We can assume that poverty had driven her back to the Palace bar and that prostitution had become her life. According to Eric, she did not feel like getting another job, which suggests she had given up hope. When we consider her hard work and potential at Birling's factory where she could have become 'a leading operator' (p. 14) we see how much she had changed and how hopeless her life must have seemed.

Using the name 'Birling' at the Brumley Women's Charity Organization was logical, since Eric was the father of her child. It also gave her some dignity. This makes Mrs Birling's refusal to help seem even more petty and unjust.

Priestley ensures that the details we learn about Eva Smith are vague. Eric did not even know her name. As her circumstances declined, the audience has the sense that her character became frail. She was becoming one of the 'millions' of anonymous poor (p. 56) whom the Inspector will refer to in his final speech. This uncertainty about her identity is also useful later on in the final act, when her very existence is questioned.

TOP TIP (A01)

Think about how Eva Smith would have been treated if she had become a member of the Birling family. From what you know, would she have been accepted or not? Make notes with evidence from the text about the characters' likely responses.

KEY CONTEXT (A03)

The use of euphemism in the *An Inspector Calls* accurately portrays the custom and values of the Edwardian period. However, the audience of 1946, when the play was first performed in London, would also have been shocked to hear the blunter word 'prostitute' used.

TOP TIP (A01)

Eric's comment, 'she was pretty and a good sport' (p. 52), is reminiscent of the kind of comment made by boys at public schools of the period, in which sport was highly valued. What does it confirm about Eric's nature?

ACT THREE, PART 3: THE INSPECTOR'S HEARTFELT WORDS (pp. 53–6)

SUMMARY

- Mr Birling tells his wife that Eric is responsible for the girl/Eva Smith's pregnancy and that he stole money from the company office.
- Mrs Birling is shocked and Eric says he intended to pay back the money.
- Mr Birling starts to plan how to cover up Eric's fraud.
- Eric tells his father that he did not feel he could ask him for help.
- Eric informs the Inspector that the girl refused the stolen money.
- Sheila explains that Mrs Birling met Eva Smith, and the Inspector explains why and how.
- Eric accuses his mother of killing her own grandchild.
- The Inspector shows how each of them helped to push the girl towards suicide. Sheila cries.
- The Inspector delivers a final speech before leaving, in which he warns what will happen if people do not accept how to live responsibly as part of a caring community.

WHY IS THIS SECTION IMPORTANT?

- **A** Eric is shown to be a **thief**, but also that he cares about what happened to the girl.
- **B** Once again Mr Birling's is concerned to **avoid scandal**.
- **C** The **guilt** of each member of the family has been demonstrated.
- **D** The Inspector becomes the **voice of morality and righteousness**.
- **E** The mood of **celebration** we saw at the start of the play is completely **destroyed**.

KEY QUOTATION: THE INSPECTOR'S WARNING (A01)

Priestley's message is summed up in the Inspector's warning to the Birlings that we all have a responsibility in society to care for each other and that 'the time will soon come when, if men will not learn that lesson, then they will be taught it in fire and blood and anguish' (p. 56). The **metaphor** 'fire and blood and anguish' is a powerful image that suggests conflict. The words 'fire', 'blood' and 'anguish' also have a religious interpretation, as if the Inspector were a prophet or holy man.

KEY CONTEXT (A03)

Some critics have said that Priestley did not need to include the Inspector's final speech, because it felt as if the Inspector was preaching at the audience. Others think that Priestley included the speech deliberately to make the audience think about their own as well as the Birlings' responsibilities. Reread the speech and decide what you think.

KEY CONTEXT (A03)

While the 1946 audience would be well aware of both the First World War (1914–18) and the Second World War (1939–45) as two of the conflicts the Inspector alludes to, they would also be aware of another conflict that Priestley would have in mind: the Russian Revolution (1917) in which the Tsar (Emperor) was overthrown by the people and replaced by Communism (common ownership).

KEY CHARACTER: ERIC'S CONTRARY NATURE (A01)

Priestley shows Eric expressing a range of feelings and character traits. We have seen Eric's initial lack of concern about Eva Smith and his immaturity. However, he does attempt to help her when she becomes pregnant. Priestley's characterisation of Eric means we believe he is motivated partly out of self-centredness and partly from a genuine concern for the girl's welfare. His denial that he truly stole the money reveals his failure to face unpleasant truths (p. 53). But his reaction to his mother's refusal to help the girl and the consequences of her actions show that Eric has a moral aspect to his character. He is stunned by Mrs Birling's behaviour and, *'nearly at breaking point'* (p. 55), accuses her of killing her unborn grandchild.

KEY STRUCTURE: DRAMATIC TENSION AND CLIMAX (A02)

Priestley brings the action to a climax when Eric accuses his mother of causing the death of Eva Smith and her unborn child. There has been a slow build-up of tension. First, we learned of Eric's relations with Eva Smith and her pregnancy, then Eric's theft of money and Mr Birling's angry reaction. Finally we see the tension culminate in Eric's explosive outburst when he learns of his mother's involvement and refusal to help the girl. This climax shows the most dramatic division yet between the values of the younger and older generations in the reactions of Eric and his mother. The climax also prepares the way for the Inspector's final, powerful polemic, the most important climax in the play.

> **TOP TIP** (A02)
>
> Mr Birling's reaction to Eric's theft is to cover up the scandal. Look back at Mr Birling's comments to Gerald on p. 8 and make notes about why they are ironic.

> **TOP TIP** (A02)
>
> Reread the Inspector's speech, starting on p. 55. He reminds the Birlings how each was a link in the chain leading to Eva Smith's death. Make notes about how each character responds and what this confirms about the older and younger Birlings.

EXAM FOCUS: WRITING ABOUT THE INSPECTOR'S SPEECH (A02)

Here is what one student has written about Inspector Goole's final speech.

> Inspector Goole's final monologue about the need for us all to support the wider community has great dramatic effect. Priestley uses several devices to do with the form of the speech that help to drive home his message. Repetition of the words, 'we' and 'millions' gives emphasis. The listing of abstract nouns such as 'hopes' and 'fears' gives a steady strong rhythm to the character's voice, as well as showing that the ordinary person can have deep feelings.

Sound use of a literary term

A good example of a device used and its effect

A good example of more than one effect

Now you try it:

Add a statement on the effect created by the *length* of the Inspector's sentences and in particular the effect of the final *two* sentences of his monologue.

TOP TIP (A02)

Sheila accuses her father of not accepting his guilt, and it is important to understand how Mr Birling separates himself and his wife from the chain of events. Find where Sheila challenges her father and outlines the chain of events again in this part of the play.

ACT THREE, PART 4: RAKING OVER THE REMAINS (pp. 57–61)

SUMMARY

- Sheila is crying, Mrs Birling has collapsed in a chair, Mr Birling pours himself a drink, swallows it quickly and turns on Eric, worried about a scandal.

- The two men argue over the stolen money. Mrs Birling declares she is ashamed of Eric who declares he is ashamed of both his parents.

- Sheila tells her parents that they are behaving as though they have learned nothing.

- Sheila questions whether or not Inspector Goole was a real police officer. This arouses her parents' interest.

- Mr Birling declares that Eric could be ruined because of the theft. He accuses his children of being fooled by the Inspector.

- Mrs Birling supports her husband, who wonders how to escape a scandal.

- Gerald returns.

WHY IS THIS SECTION IMPORTANT?

A   It shows that even when their **guilt** is established the **family** are still **divided**.

B   Sheila and Eric, who represent the young, are **united** against their parents, who represent the older generation.

C   **Questions** are raised about the Inspector's **true identity**.

KEY THEME: THE GENERATION GAP A02

Once the Inspector has gone and the Birlings are able to behave more freely, Priestley creates a dramatic situation for maximum impact. The Birlings become like two opposing armies, Sheila and Eric on one side and Mr and Mrs Birling on the other. Mr Birling remains untouched by the Inspector's words and still holds the values he had at the beginning of the play (p. 6). Mrs Birling supports her husband. Sheila and Eric's concern is a moral one, their parts in the death of the girl – the Inspector's words have struck home. However, the contrast between the generations is most striking when Sheila says to her father, 'you don't seem to have learnt anything' and Mr Birling replies, 'I've learnt plenty tonight' (p. 58). The generations no longer seem to understand each other at all. Priestley has set them against each other intentionally. He is addressing his audience, saying that if society is to change for the better after the Second World War it is the younger 'impressionable' (p. 30) generation who will make the difference.

KEY QUOTATION: THE INSPECTOR'S IDENTITY A02

Eric reminds his father of the speech he made earlier about ignoring 'cranks' (p. 58) who claim we are all responsible for each other. Eric points out that 'one of those cranks walked in – the Inspector' (p. 58). Sheila asks if the Inspector arrived at this point. The audience is thus alerted to the possibility that the Inspector is not who he says he is – even that he is some kind of supernatural being who has come with a purpose: to teach these people a lesson about social responsibility.

TOP TIP A04

You need to embed your quotations within your sentences to support what you write, so make sure your quotations are not too long.

CHECKPOINT 9 A01

Sum up how the different characters view the importance of the Inspector's status as a police officer.

EXAM FOCUS: WRITING ABOUT DIFFERENT VIEWPOINTS A01

Here is what one student has written about the way characters respond differently to the possibility that the Inspector is an imposter.

> Priestley shows us that for Sheila and Eric, 'it doesn't make any real difference' whether the Inspector was a real police officer or not because he has made them face what they did to Eva Smith. By contrast, for Mr and Mrs Birling, whether he was an imposter 'matters a devil of a lot' because only a real police officer could take action against them. Both Sheila and Eric have faced the truth about their own self-centredness and lack of concern for others.

Quotation embedded in the text

A clear contrast is made between the characters' responses

A key point showing the characters' similar attitudes

Now you try it:

Add a statement showing how Mr and Mrs Birling's view contrasts with Sheila and Eric's.

ACT THREE, PART 5: THREE TELEPHONE CALLS (pp. 61–72)

SUMMARY

- Sheila tries to bring Gerald up to date, but her parents prevent her.
- Gerald has discovered that the Inspector is almost certainly not a police officer. Mr Birling rings Chief Constable Roberts and confirms that there is no Inspector Goole.
- Sheila objects to her parents' triumphant attitude. Eric agrees.
- Mr Birling thinks the visit was a hoax. He considers how to avoid a scandal. Eric reminds him that a girl died. Sheila supports Eric. Mr Birling reminds Eric of the theft.
- Gerald wonders if Eva Smith actually existed. They question whether the photograph was the same each time it was seen.
- Gerald rings the Infirmary. There have been no recent suicides and nobody has been admitted after drinking disinfectant.
- Sheila remembers the Inspector's words, but Mr Birling dismisses her.
- Gerald tries to persuade Sheila to take back the ring, but she needs time to think.
- The telephone rings. Mr Birling answers. A girl has just died after committing suicide. An Inspector is on his way to interview them.

WHY IS THIS SECTION IMPORTANT?

A It seems Inspector Goole is **not** a real **police officer**.

B **Questions** are asked as to **whether Eva Smith is a real person** and whether the family had dealings with the **same girl**.

C The **tension decreases** when there appears to have been no suicide. Mr and Mrs Birling **feel no guilt** for their past actions.

D The **rift** between the **younger** and **older Birlings grows**. Sheila and Eric's **attitude** is **contrasted** with that of the **other three**.

E We are led towards the **dramatic final twist**.

TOP TIP (A01)

If a question asks you to 'compare' or 'contrast', make sure you answer appropriately. For example, find references or quotations in this section that contrast Sheila's and Gerald's attitude to the Inspector.

TOP TIP (A02)

Notice how, in discrediting the Inspector, Gerald conveniently forgets about his treatment of the girl and his deception of Sheila. If we look at Gerald's attitude in other situations we can see a pattern (see pp. 63 and 71). Gerald likes to avoid unpleasant truths. In this respect, he is not unlike Eric.

KEY STRUCTURE: A PATTERN OF MOOD CHANGES (A02)

Priestley structures the events to create different moods. As the characters assess the Inspector's story and work out the details, the tension lessens. Priestley leads the audience to believe, as Mr Birling says, 'no police enquiry. No one girl that all this happened to. No scandal' (p. 69). Then, just as they think all is well, the telephone rings. The mood suddenly shifts to apprehension. The characters 'stare guiltily and dumbfounded' (p. 72) as Mr Birling declares that a police Inspector is on his way. The audience, as well as the characters, are taken completely by surprise. The question of the Inspector's identity is reopened. We are taken back to the beginning of the play to ask: What will happen now? How will the characters behave this time? What will the consequences be? The final twist was described at the time as 'the best coup de théâtre of the year'.

TOP TIP (A03)

To fully appreciate a play you should see it performed. If you can't see a theatre production of *An Inspector Calls*, try to see a television production or a film. You can also read the play aloud in your own time with a group of other students, each taking and swapping roles.

CHECKPOINT 10 (A01)

How do their reactions at this point in the play make Sheila and Eric different from the others?

EXAM FOCUS: WRITING ABOUT SHEILA AND ERIC'S FEAR (A02)

Here is what one student has written on the effects of Sheila and Eric's viewpoint.

> Towards the end of the play, Priestley shows us how Sheila and Eric's bitterness and anger at the way they could so easily forget the Inspector's words turns to fear. Sheila remembers how the Inspector made her 'feel' and she repeats the Inspector's words, 'fire and blood and anguish'. The effect of this metaphor on the 1946 audience would be to remind them of two world wars.

Important shift in mood mentioned

Good use of literary technique

Shows the effect on the audience

Now you try it:

Add a statement showing how Sheila and Eric's fear is a warning. Start: *So the audience would see that ...*

PROGRESS AND REVISION CHECK

SECTION ONE: CHECK YOUR KNOWLEDGE

Answer these quick questions to test your basic knowledge of the play, its characters and events:

1. Who agrees with Mr Birling's assessment that 'increasing prosperity' (p. 6) is to come?

2. Who says there is 'nothing to gain by war'? (p. 6)

3. How did Eva Smith die?

4. Why did Mr Birling refuse to increase his workers' pay?

5. Who tells us Eva Smith found a job at Milwards shop?

6. What two characters in Act One are shown the photograph of Eva Smith?

7. What does Sheila warn Gerald not to do at the end of Act One?

8. Who refers to Eva Smith as a girl 'of that class' (p. 30) and what does she mean?

9. Who tells Mrs Birling about Eric's drinking and who confirms it?

10. When did Gerald meet Daisy Renton and when did the affair end?

11. How does the Inspector know that Daisy Renton went to the seaside?

12. What is the purpose of the Brumley Women's Charity Organization?

13. Who does Mrs Birling think should be held responsible for Eva Smith's pregnancy?

14. When did Eric meet 'this girl' (p. 51) at the Place Theatre bar?

15. How much did Eric steal from Birling's office?

16. Who does the Inspector say helped to kill Eva Smith?

17. Who does Mr Birling ring to find out if there is an Inspector Goole?

18. Who establishes that there was no recent suicide?

19. What image from the Inspector's speech sticks in Sheila's mind?

20. Who answers the final phone call and who else is present when it is answered?

PROGRESS AND REVISION CHECK

SECTION TWO: CHECK YOUR UNDERSTANDING

Here are two tasks about the significance of particular moments in the play. These require more thought and slightly longer responses. In each case, try to write at least three to four paragraphs.

Task 1: Why are the sections in which Sheila's engagement ring is discussed significant (pp. 5, 40, 71–72)? Think about:

- Sheila's changing attitude to Gerald
- What Sheila learns about herself

Task 2: Why is Mr Birling's speech about the future (pp. 6–7) important? Think about:

- What it tells you about Mr Birling's judgement about progress in business and manufacturing
- What it tells you about his judgement about the future of society

PROGRESS CHECK

GOOD PROGRESS

I can:
- understand how Priestley has sequenced and revealed events. ☐
- refer to the importance of key events in the play. ☐
- select well-chosen evidence, including key quotations, to support my ideas. ☐

EXCELLENT PROGRESS

I can:
- refer in depth to main and minor events and how they contribute to the development of the plot. ☐
- understand how Priestley has carefully ordered or revealed events for particular effects. ☐
- draw on a range of carefully selected key evidence, including quotations, to support my ideas. ☐

WHO'S WHO?

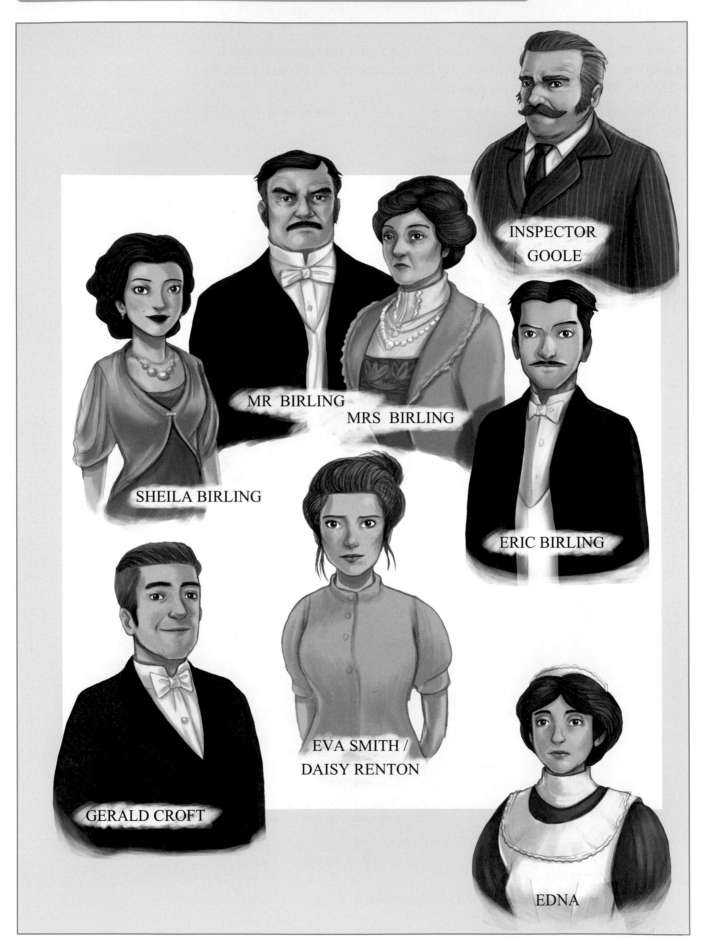

INSPECTOR GOOLE

SHEILA BIRLING

MR BIRLING

MRS BIRLING

ERIC BIRLING

GERALD CROFT

EVA SMITH / DAISY RENTON

EDNA

EVA SMITH/DAISY RENTON

EVA SMITH/DAISY RENTON'S ROLE IN THE PLAY

Eva Smith, also known as Daisy Renton, is the young woman who suffered at the hands of the Birling family and Gerald. She does not appear in the play. We are told that she:

- was sacked by Mr Birling from his factory for leading a strike for better pay.
- was sacked from a dress shop after Sheila unjustly complained about her.
- became the mistress of Gerald Croft to whom she was known as Daisy Renton.
- was made pregnant by Eric Birling.
- applied to a charity for help, but Mrs Birling refused her.
- committed suicide by swallowing disinfectant.

EXAM FOCUS: WRITING ABOUT EVA SMITH

Key point	Evidence/Further meaning
• Being bred in the country meant Eva Smith was more naive than a city girl. However, she was capable of doing well.	• 'a lively good-looking girl – country bred' and a 'good worker too' (Mr Birling, p. 14) • Reveals that Mr Birling recalls Eva Smith as a pretty girl from the countryside who knew how to work hard.
• She was capable of being a leader.	• 'She'd had a lot to say – far too much – so she had to go.' (Mr Birling, p. 15) • Reveals she was not afraid to speak up (on behalf of others) for more pay. Consequently she was dismissed.
• She seemed experienced and consequently less naive than she was.	• 'she was very pretty and looked as if she could take care of herself' (Sheila, p. 24) • Reveals that Sheila judged the girl by her appearance, and wrongly assumed she would find other work.
• Without work her prospects declined.	• 'Now she had to try something else.' (Inspector, p. 25) • Without legitimate work she had to turn to 'something else', a euphemism for prostitution.

THE INSPECTOR

THE INSPECTOR'S ROLE IN THE PLAY

Inspector Goole presents himself to the Birlings and Gerald as a police officer who has come to investigate the suicide of a young woman, Eva Smith. During the play he:

- interrupts the celebratory dinner.
- questions each of the other characters in turn.
- establishes that each had an unwitting part in Eva Smith's death, through either cruelty or disregard for her welfare.
- gradually takes more control of the situation and has little regard for social class or status.
- is concerned about honesty and justice.
- makes a powerful speech about our responsibility to each other in the wider society.

THE INSPECTOR'S IMPORTANCE TO THE PLAY AS A WHOLE

Priestley uses the character of Inspector Goole to present his ideas about the need for a just society and a communal sense of responsibility. As well as increasingly governing events at the Birling house, the Inspector also links all the characters to the 'chain of events' (p. 14) that culminates in Eva Smith's suicide.

TOP TIP (A01)

Make sure that you note how the Inspector controls events and why. Ask yourself: What are your first impressions of him? How does he regard the Birlings and Gerald? How does his control increase as the play develops? What is the purpose of his visit?

TOP TIP (A02)

Note the way Priestley presents the relationship between Chief Constable Colonel Roberts and Mr Birling, then ask yourself: How is Inspector Goole different? Why does Mr Birling think the Inspector would not 'play golf' (p. 16)? Why does the Inspector ignore Mr Birling's demands (p. 17)?

EXAM FOCUS: WRITING ABOUT THE INSPECTOR

Key point	Evidence/Further meaning
● The Inspector is an imposing figure who will dominate the play and will achieve his aims.	● He is a man of 'massiveness, solidity and purposefulness' (p. 11). ● Shows how the Inspector's physical presence matches his identity.
● He likes to do things in an orderly way. This allows J. B. Priestley to build the play as a 'chain of events' (p. 14).	● 'One person and one line of enquiry at a time. Otherwise, there's a muddle.' (p. 12) ● Indicates that all the Birlings and Gerald are involved in the inquiries.
● The Inspector has high moral standards, revealing that the others characters have not.	● 'It's my duty to ask questions.' (p. 15) ● He takes his responsibilities seriously.
● The inspector's distinctive and mysterious presence sets him apart from the other characters.	● 'He never seemed like an ordinary police inspector' (p. 59). ● Suggests he was different in some way or that he was somehow 'extraordinary', more than human.

TOP TIP: 'GOOLE' OR 'GHOUL' (A01)

Note the Inspector's key character traits, in particular his single mindedness when questioning the characters and ability to overrule them (Act One, pp. 12, 17, 21–3; Act Two, p. 30; Act Three p. 51, 56); his power and magnetism (Act One, pp. 11, 26; Act Two, pp. 30, 37); his oratory (Act Three, p. 56) and the way in which he affects Sheila and Eric so that they confront their actions (Act One, pp. 19, 20, 23; Act Three, pp. 58, 59).

Also consider his name, 'Goole', a homophone for 'ghoul', suggesting a phantom and also a morbid interest in death, reminding us that his concern is Eva Smith's death. The Inspector's origins are unknown. Remember that Gerald discovers from a police sergeant that there is no Inspector Goole on the force (Act Three, p. 63) and this is confirmed by Mr Birling when he rings Chief Constable Colonel Roberts (pp. 62–3). The audience is, therefore, bound to ask themselves: who or what is Inspector Goole?

TOP TIP (A01)

Look at the stage directions. They give additional information to the actors. What do the stage directions tell you about Inspector Goole?

MR BIRLING

MR BIRLING'S ROLE IN THE PLAY

Mr Birling, the father of Sheila and Eric, is a wealthy businessman who owns a factory in Brumley. He has been the city's lord mayor and is a magistrate. During the play he:

- hosts a celebratory dinner for Sheila's engagement to Gerald Croft.
- is keen for the Birlings and Crofts to unite in business as well as marriage.
- is keen to receive a knighthood.
- says that a man's responsibility is only to himself and his family and not to the wider community.
- reveals that he dismissed Eva Smith from her job at his factory two years previously.
- tries to take control when the Inspector arrives, but fails.
- fears scandal and tries to protect himself and his family from involvement with Eva Smith.
- takes the final telephone call at the end of the play.

MR BIRLING'S IMPORTANCE TO THE PLAY AS A WHOLE

Arthur Birling believes that the individual has responsibilities only to himself and his family. In business his aim is to make a profit, and if this is at the expense of his workers, so be it. Although he has gained public office as a mayor and an alderman, he does not feel a responsibility to give anything back to the community. His views are the opposite of Inspector Goole's.

KEY CONTEXT **A03**

For Priestley, a socialist, Mr Birling stands for all that is wrong with Edwardian society because he does not use his power and wealth to help create social justice.

KEY CONTEXT **A03**

In 1912 trade unions were not well established and many employers did not take them seriously. Consequently, Mr Birling could easily dismiss workers such as Eva Smith.

EXAM FOCUS: WRITING ABOUT MR BIRLING

A01

Key point	Evidence/Further meaning
● Mr Birling's size helps to give him a threatening appearance.	● *'heavy-looking, rather portentous man'* (p. 1) ● Reveals him as a thickset, pompous man.
● He doesn't let sentiment get in the way of whatever needs to be done to succeed.	● 'a hard-headed, practical man of business' (p. 6) ● He thinks of himself as a man who does well in business.
● Suggests he has a high opinion of his own importance.	● 'Yes, my dear, I know – I'm talking too much.' (p. 7) ● He likes to air his views and is aware that he tends to monopolise the conversation.
● He expects others to acknowledge his importance and show respect.	● 'I'm a public man' (p. 41) ● He has been in positions of power, locally, as a member of the town council and Lord Mayor, and is still a magistrate.

TOP TIP: POSITION AND POWER

A01

Ensure that you show how Priestley presents Mr Birling as a powerful man (Act One, p. 11; Act Two, p. 31) full of his own importance (Act One, p. 11) who tries to intimidate the Inspector (Act One, p. 17). Note the way Mr Birling declares his views at the beginning of the play (Act One, pp. 6, 10). Despite hearing of Eva Smith's suicide he shows no remorse for his part in her decline (Act Three pp. 57, 58). He continually strives to protect himself and his family from scandal (Act Two, p. 45; Act Three, pp. 54, 58) and from losing his chance of a knighthood (Act Three p. 57).

AIMING HIGH: CHARACTER DEVELOPMENT

★

For higher grades, it's important that you can write about the way Priestley presents Mr Birling as the play progresses. To develop your views, try asking yourself the following questions. How is he presented initially? What are his views? What is his relationship like with the other Birlings and Gerald? What is his response to the Inspector as the play develops? What is he most afraid of? How does he behave when the Inspector leaves?

MRS BIRLING

MRS BIRLING'S ROLE IN THE PLAY

Mrs Birling is the wife of Mr Birling and the mother of Sheila and Eric. She is a prominent member of the Brumley Women's Charity Organization. During the play she:

- commends Gerald's timing after he presents Sheila with an engagement ring.
- adopts a superior tone with the Inspector.
- is disgusted when she learns that Daisy Renton was Gerald's mistress, but forgets about it when she thinks a scandal has been avoided.
- uses her influence to prevent the pregnant Eva Smith receiving help from the charity.
- thinks Eva Smith and the father of the unborn child are to blame for Eva Smith's death, before she realises that Eric is the father.

- claims she was the only one who stood up to the Inspector's questioning.

TOP TIP (A01)

Note the way Priestley builds the dramatic tension around Mrs Birling as the Inspector questions her. What does she reveal about her attitude to Eva Smith? Why does Sheila try to stop her mother talking? What does Mrs Birling discover?

EXAM FOCUS: WRITING ABOUT MRS BIRLING

Key point	Evidence/Further meaning
• Mrs Birling regards most people as beneath her and expects the Inspector to treat her with respect.	• *'a rather cold woman and her husband's social superior'* (p. 1) • Mrs Birling is not a friendly person and rarely shows any affection. She comes from a higher social class than her husband's.
• She is used to being listened to and having her opinions accepted as right.	• *'Please don't contradict me like that.'* (p. 30) • She does not like, and doesn't expect, people to disagree with her.
• She is prudish, unforgiving and intolerant of people's mistakes.	• *'It's disgusting to me.'* (p. 38) • Even though Gerald comes from a good family and meets with her approval as a future son-in-law, she cannot accept Gerald's affair.
• She is able to influence the decisions the charity organisation makes.	• *'the most prominent member of the committee'* (pp. 43–4) • She is the most powerful and respected member of the group that runs the charity.

ERIC BIRLING

ERIC'S ROLE IN THE PLAY

Eric Birling is the son of Mr and Mrs Birling and brother to Sheila. He works in his father's firm. During the play he:

- drinks too much at the celebratory dinner.
- admits that he made Eva Smith pregnant after meeting her at the Palace Theatre.
- admits he gave Eva Smith money that he stole from his father's firm.
- accuses his mother of murdering his unborn child and her grandchild.
- acknowledges his irresponsibility towards Eva Smith and accepts the Inspector's words.

EXAM FOCUS: WRITING ABOUT ERIC BIRLING (A01)

Key point	Evidence/Further meaning
● Eric is treated as an irresponsible child by his father.	● 'Just keep quiet, Eric, and don't get excited' (p. 13) ● Reveals that Mr Birling knows that Eric has drunk too much and might say something he shouldn't.
● Mr Birling feels he knows more of life than his son.	● 'That's something this public-school-and-Varsity life you've had doesn't seem to teach you.' (p. 16) ● Reveals Eric has been educated at an expensive school and university. Suggests Mr Birling hasn't.
● Eric doesn't discuss his problems or private life with his mother.	● 'you're not the type – you don't get drunk' (p. 50) ● We know that Eric does get drunk, and that the opposite of what his mother says is true.
● Eric's immaturity.	● 'Your trouble is – you've been spoilt' (p. 54) ● Mr Birling thinks that by being the boss's son Eric has had too easy a life.

TOP TIP: ERIC REGRETS (A01)

Eric's change is not as profound as Sheila's, but he is greatly affected by the Inspector's words. Show how Priestley presents him as a character ill at ease with others (Act One, p. 3) who drinks too much (Act One, p. 3; Act Three, p. 51). Explain how he is troubled by Eva Smith's suicide (Act Three, p. 55) and the death of his unborn child (Act Three, p. 55), the way he is affected by the Inspector's words (Act Three, pp. 58, 59, 64) and recognises his guilt (Act Three, p. 64). By contrast, show his attitude to the theft from his father's firm (Act Three, p. 53) and his unhappiness with his parents (pp. 54, 55). Finally, decide if there are any indications that Eric's behaviour is likely to change (Act Three, pp. 64, 65, 68–9, 71).

TOP TIP (A01)

Compare and contrast Priestley's presentation of Eric with his presentation of Gerald. What are their similarities and differences at the beginning of the play and at the end of the play?

SHEILA BIRLING

SHEILA'S ROLE IN THE PLAY

Sheila Birling is the daughter of Mr and Mrs Birling and sister to Eric. She is engaged to Gerald Croft. During the play she:

- is initially pleased and excited at the prospect of her marriage.
- is distressed when she hears that a young woman, Eva Smith, has taken her own life.
- reveals that she was responsible for Eva Smith's dismissal from Milwards shop .
- recognises Inspector Goole cannot be lied to.
- breaks off her engagement to Gerald when she discovers he had an affair with Daisy Renton/Eva Smith.
- reveals that Eric drinks too much.
- acknowledges her part in Eva Smith's downfall and takes the Inspector's words to heart.

KEY CONTEXT (A03)

Edwardian middle- and upper-class parents often encouraged or sometimes forced their sons and daughters to marry for money. Sheila and Gerald are a love match, although Mr Birling also has a keen eye on the financial rewards the marriage will bring.

SHEILA'S IMPORTANCE TO THE PLAY AS A WHOLE

Of all the **characters**, Sheila changes the most. She is greatly troubled when she realises that her petty jealously at Milwards meant such hardship for Eva Smith. She respects Gerald's honesty about his affair, but also has the courage to break off her engagement to him. Most importantly, she is affected by the Inspector's words. Her focus on frivolous concerns shifts, and she supports the need for social justice. For Priestley, Sheila represents the belief that young people are open to change.

TOP TIP: WRITING ABOUT SHEILA'S VOICE (A01)

Note Sheila's voice at the beginning of Act One when we first meet her at the dinner table. She is lively, chiding Gerald, 'I should jolly well think not' (p. 2), or adopts a 'mock aggressiveness' (p. 3), 'Gerald – just you object!' (p. 3) as though she has no cares. Although she protests that Gerald neglected her the previous year, her overall mood at this time is carefree. This allows Priestley to create a dramatic contrast in Sheila's voice and mood after the Inspector arrives, and you can find numerous examples of how her light heartedness has changed to distress, scorn or anxiety as Eva Smith's story unfolds (pp. 17, 38, 71).

EXAM FOCUS: WRITING ABOUT SHEILA BIRLING

Key point	Evidence/Further meaning
• Sheila feels shock at the death of a young woman, revealing that she can't imagine someone not having a lot to live for.	• 'Oh – how horrible! Was it an accident?' (p. 17) • Shows her naivety to assume that someone could drink a fatal amount of disinfectant 'by accident'.
• Although bitter, her curiosity needs to be satisfied and she is strong enough to hear the full story.	• 'I wouldn't miss it for worlds' (p. 34) • Reveals her bitterness at Gerald's affair.
• She is strong enough to accept responsibility for what she has done and to feel regret.	• 'I had her turned out of a job.' (p. 56) • Shows she can confront her bad behaviour.
• Sheila believes that it doesn't matter whether the Inspector is a real police officer or not. She is only concerned that they all harmed someone.	• 'it's you two who are being childish – trying not to face the facts' (p. 59) • She recognises her parents' faults and their failure to acknowledge them.

TOP TIP: SHEILA'S PROGRESS

Show how Priestley presents Sheila's development as the character that changes the most. At first she is playful and egotistical (Act One, pp. 2–5), but becomes serious and troubled at the news of a young woman's death (Act One, pp. 17, 19). She questions her own behaviour and regrets her treatment of Eva Smith (Act One, p. 24; Act Three, p. 57). Explain how she reproaches Gerald (Act One, p. 26; Act Two, pp. 34, 38, 40), but keeps the way open for a possible reconciliation (Act Three, p. 72). Sheila fully accepts the Inspector's words (Act Three, pp. 58, 59) and is distressed when her parents do not (Act Three, pp. 57, 71).

TOP TIP

Note the way Priestley presents Sheila. What does she care about, initially? How does her mood change? How do her views change and why? How does her relationship with Gerald change? How does her relationship with Eric change? What does she think of her parents by the end of the play?

GERALD CROFT

GERALD'S ROLE IN THE PLAY

Gerald, who is the son of a wealthy industrialist and rival of Birling's, has become engaged to Sheila. During the play he:

- gives Sheila the engagement ring during the celebratory dinner.
- shows he has the same approach to business as Mr Birling.
- conducts himself agreeably and politely with Mr and Mrs Birling.
- tells how he rescued Daisy Renton/Eva Smith from the drunken Alderman Meggarty.
- admits that he kept the girl as his secret mistress for six months, then broke off their relationship.
- discovers that a police sergeant has never heard of an Inspector Goole.
- telephones the Infirmary and learns that no girl died that day.

EXAM FOCUS: WRITING ABOUT GERALD CROFT (A01)

Key point	Evidence/Further meaning
• Gerald is self-assured, mature and worldly wise.	• *'easy, well-bred young man-about-town'* (p. 2) • Reveals that Gerald is upper class and has a polite, relaxed manner.
• Mr Birling thinks that Gerald will make a good business partner as well as a husband for Sheila.	• 'You're just the kind of son-in-law I always wanted.' (p. 4) • Reveals that Mr Birling sees Gerald as being like himself – a determined man of business.
• Gerald can maintain a stiff upper lip while being troubled by Daisy Renton/Eva Smith's suicide.	• 'I'm rather more – upset – by this business than I probably appear to be' (p. 39) • Deep down Gerald is greatly saddened by the girl's death and feels in part responsible.
• Gerald has double standards. When he thinks a scandal has been averted, he wants to resume his engagement, forgetting that he abandoned Daisy Renton/Eva Smith.	• 'Everything's all right now, Sheila. (*Holds up the ring.*) What about this ring?' (p. 71) • Shows Gerald wants to continue his relationship with Sheila.

PROGRESS AND REVISION CHECK

SECTION ONE: CHECK YOUR KNOWLEDGE

Answer these quick questions to test your basic knowledge of the play's characters.

1. Who is described as 'half shy, half assertive', who as 'very pleased with life' and who as a 'young man-about-town'?

2. What were the different names used by the girl who committed suicide?

3. What impression do we get of Mrs Birling when we first meet her?

4. How would you describe Mr Birling when he discovers that the Inspector is an imposter?

5. What impression does the Inspector's physical appearance create?

6. What character has the fewest lines to speak in the play?

7. Who is the alderman who visited the Palace Theatre bar?

8. What servants do the Birlings employ?

9. Who is absent from the engagement dinner?

10. What is the name and title of Mr Birling's friend in the police force?

SECTION TWO: CHECK YOUR UNDERSTANDING

Here is a task about Inspector Goole. This requires more thought and a slightly longer response. Try to write at least three to four paragraphs.

Task: How does Inspector Goole speak to the other characters? Think about:

- His physical manner and how he questions them
- How his manner changes over the course of the play and why

PROGRESS CHECK

GOOD PROGRESS

I can:
- explain the significance of the main characters in how the action develops. ☐
- refer to how they are described by Priestley and how this affects the way we see them. ☐

EXCELLENT PROGRESS

I can:
- analyse in detail how Priestley has shaped and developed characters over the course of the play. ☐
- infer key ideas, themes and issues from the ways characters and relationships are presented by Priestley. ☐

THEME TRACKER A01

Equality

- p. 8: Mr Birling shows his belief in the class structure by acknowledging Lady Croft's superior position.
- pp. 15, 16: Mr Birling explains why he dismissed the strikers. Gerald agrees. Eric disagrees.
- p. 41: Sheila challenges her mother's belief in their superior social position.

THEMES

EQUALITY

Priestley presents the audience with a powerful social and political message. The Inspector is his mouthpiece. He is the character who highlights the inequalities in society. Make sure you remember:

- The comfortable life of the middle-class Birlings (pp. 1, 2) is compared with the lives of their working-class employees (p. 15).
- The Inspector highlights injustices and inequalities. He makes his point more and more forcefully as the play progresses. In his final **monologue** he says that if injustice is allowed to continue it will lead to dreadful consequences – to 'fire and blood and anguish' (p. 56).
- Sheila and Eric are affected by the Inspector's words and are fearful of what the future will bring if society does not change (p. 71).
- Priestley is saying that hope for a more just society lies with the younger generation. The young are not set in their ways like the older generation, but are 'more impressionable' (p. 30) according to the Inspector.

EXAM FOCUS: WRITING ABOUT EFFECTS

Here is what one student has written about the way Priestley presents Sheila's attitude to working-class women. It also shows the difference between Sheila and Eva Smith's position in society.

> Early on in the play, Sheila is outraged at factory owners, such as her father, employing young women cheaply and points out that they aren't 'cheap labour' but 'people'. However, Sheila is capable of treating such women badly, too. Out of jealousy, she told the manager at Milwards to dismiss Eva Smith (the sales assistant) because the dress Sheila liked suited Eva better. The effect Priestley wants to create is that Sheila is not a truly bad person, but she is ignorant. Sheila takes for granted that because she comes from a powerful Brumley family she can do as she wants and 'get rid of' people like Eva Smith, without thinking about the consequences.

Reveals an aspect of Sheila's character

Introduces a contradictory side to Sheila's character

Shows clearly the effect created by the writer

Points to unequal social positions

Now you try it:

Add a final sentence saying how Sheila feels when she realises the consequences of her power over Eva Smith.

RESPONSIBILITY

The **theme** of responsibility is closely related to the theme of equality and occurs in different ways throughout the play:

- Mr Birling feels his responsibility is to make as large a profit as he can from his business, whether or not this means treating his workers unfairly (p. 15).
- Mrs Birling has responsibilities as chair of the Brumley Women's Charity Organization, but believes that help should only be given to those who deserve it (pp. 42, 44).
- Sheila realises too late that her social standing as a valued Milwards' customer brings responsibilities with it.
- Eric has little sense of responsibility at all, until he is moved by the Inspector's words (pp. 64, 65).
- Gerald showed some responsibility by helping Daisy Renton escape from the Palace Theatre bar. He provided for her to a limited extent, but he also disregarded his responsibilities to Sheila.

Remember that the main focus of responsibility in the play is that which the Birlings and Gerald had to Eva Smith, and how their failure to take responsibility decided her fate:

- Mr Birling dismissed her from his factory.
- Sheila had her dismissed from Milwards.
- Eric and Gerald took advantage of her vulnerability.
- Mrs Birling refused to help her when she most needed it.

AIMING HIGH: COMMENT ON EDNA

Through Inspector Goole Priestley emphasises the Birlings' responsibilities to the wider community by focusing on their treatment of Eva Smith. To gain higher marks you could also discuss Edna, the maid, and the Birlings' attitude to her, bearing in mind that domestic servants relied on the goodwill of their employers and could be dismissed without justification or compensation.

Edna is a very minor character in the play with few lines, most of which include the words 'Ma'am' (p. 2) or 'sir' (p. 10) and illustrate her lowly status and her employers' superiority. There is no conversation between Edna and the Birlings. Priestley has deliberately given Edna little dialogue and no character development for particular effects. He is making the point that she is one of the invisible 'millions of Eva Smiths and John Smiths' (p. 56). We do not know what Edna's hopes and fears are. Nor, it is safe to say, would Mr and Mrs Birling. They are unlikely to feel any responsibility to her beyond paying her wages. Also note how Edna ushers Inspector Goole into the dining room (p. 10), a fitting action, since he is about to address the Birlings on their responsibility to women like her.

THEME TRACKER A01

Responsibility

- pp. 10, 58: Mr Birling gives a speech about responsibility to oneself and one's family, and Eric later remarks on it.
- p. 48: Mrs Birling states her view about who is to blame for Eva Smith's pregnancy.
- p. 56: Inspector Goole gives an impassioned speech on responsibility to others.

KEY CONTEXT A03

Servants like Edna worked very long hours, usually rising between five and six in the morning and finishishing work at any time, depending on the requirements of their employers. Note how Mrs Birling asks Edna 'to wait up' (p. 61) to make tea for the family.

THEME TRACKER (A01)

Love and marriage

- p. 8: The family toasts Sheila and Gerald's engagement.
- p. 38: Sheila demands to know if Gerald loved Daisy Renton. Gerald is uncertain.
- p. 72: Sheila no longer knows what her feelings are for Gerald. She needs to understand everything that has happened before she can resume the engagement.

LOVE AND MARRIAGE

Priestley explores the nature of love and marriage from the perspectives of different **characters** and, in some cases, how their understanding of love changes:

- Mr Birling sees marriage as a way of climbing the social ladder, so he is delighted at Sheila's engagement to Gerald, the son of a Lord.
- Mr Birling's motives for marrying Sybil Birling may have been more to do with her social position than with love, since she comes from a family socially superior to his.
- Parental love is lacking in Eric's life. He complains that neither of his parents are the kind he would seek help from if he was in trouble (pp. 54, 55).
- Physical attraction was one motive behind Gerald's and also Eric's relationship with Daisy Renton. She seems to have loved Gerald (p. 38) and regarded Eric as immature (p. 53).

Inspector Goole promotes love as charity, where we demonstrate care and humanity towards others in the community at large.

The love between Sheila and Gerald undergoes the greatest change:

- At the beginning of the play Sheila and Gerald appear to be romantically in love as they celebrate their engagement.
- As revelations about Gerald's affair with Daisy Renton come to light, Sheila questions whether the Gerald she loves is the one she knows. She realises that trust and honesty are the basis of a sound marriage (p. 40).

KEY QUOTATION: MR AND MRS BIRLING'S MARRIAGE (A01)

While Mr and Mrs Birling have a marriage in which they share and support each other's opinions, Mrs Birling notes that men 'with important work to do', such as her husband, 'spend nearly all their time and energy on their business' (p. 3). It suggests that the marriage lacks affection.

KEY CONTEXT (A03)

Whether or not Mrs Birling objected to her husband spending so much time on his business, she comments that when Sheila marries Gerald she'll 'have to get used to it' (p. 3). Married women during the Edwardian period, from whatever class they came, would be expected to put their husbands before themselves at all times.

REVISION FOCUS: GERALD, ERIC AND DAISY RENTON

- Reread Gerald's account of his time with Daisy Renton (pp. 34–40). Then reread Eric's account (pp. 51–4).
- Create a two-column table headed 'Gerald, Eric and Daisy Renton'. Add two subheadings: 'Similarities' and 'Differences'.
- Under the first column, write down the similarities between Gerald and Eric's treatment of Daisy Renton, making a note of any useful quotations or references.
- In the second column, carry out a similar task noting the differences between Gerald and Eric's treatment of her. Again, make a note of any useful quotations or references.

TIME

Priestley draws on ideas about time to create twists and surprises in the play. For example, the idea of time repeating itself, and using knowledge of the past to change the future, occurs at the end of the play. Here, the phone call telling the Birlings that a girl has just died brings the characters full circle. This means that:

- Inspector Goole arrives at the Birlings' to question the characters before the suicide has been discovered.
- The characters are given a chance to see the consequences of their past actions.
- The characters can change how they will react when an inspector questions them the second time round.
- At the end of the play the audience is left to consider how each character will respond. We expect Sheila and Eric to understand what they have done to Eva Smith and behave differently in the future. We expect Mr and Mrs Birling to deny any responsibility for their actions.
- It is trickier to decide what Gerald will do. His past behaviour troubles him, but how far his future behaviour would change is an open question.

AIMING HIGH: COMMENT ON THE TIMING OF THE PLAY ⭐

To show your understanding more fully, you can also discuss the timing of the play, both the period in which Priestley chose to set it (1912) and its relationship to the audience who would first see it. He set it just before the 'fire and blood and anguish' (p. 56) of the First World War (1914–18) for an audience who would have just come through the Second World War (1939–45). From Priestley's point of view it would give greater power to his words. He was appealing to the audience to consider the failure of the older generation (exemplified by Mr and Mrs Birling) to learn from their mistakes after the First World War and not to repeat this failure now the Second World War was over.

The audience would also recognise how Eric's fear of the future foreshadowed the coming loss of life among his generation. (Remember that both Eric and Gerald are of the generation that would fight in the First World War.) Also note how Eric, early on in the play, seems to challenge his father's views about the possibility of war. His father silences him (p. 6), which we could see as a symbol of the older generation failing the young. Gerald, on the other hand, agrees with Mr Birling that the future looks like 'a time of steadily increasing prosperity' (p. 6); comments that prove to be tragically ironic.

THEME TRACKER A01

Time

- p. 11: Inspector Goole informs Gerald and the Birlings that a young woman has committed suicide by drinking disinfectant.
- pp. 58–70: When the Inspector leaves, Gerald and the Birlings discover that there is no one called Inspector Goole and no recent suicide.
- p. 72: The final phone call reveals that an inspector is on his way to investigate the suicide of a young woman. Events are about to repeat themselves.

KEY CONTEXT A03

Priestley wrote several 'Time Plays', such as *Dangerous Corner* (1932) and *Time and the Conways* (1937). Like *An Inspector Calls*, there are shifts in time so the future is revealed.

KEY CONTEXT A03

Time shifts like those in *An Inspector Calls* occur in several films. For example, *Back to the Future* uses the idea of travelling back in time and ahead into the future. *Groundhog Day* uses the notion of time being circular and a particular day repeating itself.

CONTEXTS

J. B. PRIESTLEY

Here are a few key dates from J. B. Priestley's life. Remember that if you include details about the life of the author in your essay, you must make them relevant to the play:

- 1894 John Boynton Priestley is born in Bradford, Yorkshire, into a middle-class suburban family. His mother dies and his father, who becomes a headteacher, remarries.
- 1910 Priestley leaves school at 16 and takes a job as a clerk in a wool company to have time to write, rather than go on to university. At this time, his father's socialist friends influence his later views, which emerge in his writing.
- 1914–18 Aged twenty, he leaves to fight in the First World War, in the Duke of Wellington's Regiment. He is badly wounded and gassed. The experience affects his views and writing.
- 1922 He attends Trinity Hall, Cambridge University and achieves a degree.
- 1922 He works in London as a journalist and publishes his first collection of essays *Brief Diversions.* He begins his career as a successful writer.
- 1934 He writes *English Journey*, which depicts the poor in England during the economic depression.
- 1939–45 He makes regular wartime broadcasts for the BBC.
- 1945 He writes *An Inspector Calls,* the most famous of his plays.
- 1984 He dies at the age of eighty-nine, having written numerous plays, novels, essays, social history, literary criticism and an autobiography.

As a socialist, Priestley was particularly dismayed at the period between the two world wars that brought widespread poverty, economic depression and political extremism to many countries. *An Inspector Calls* is a plea for a fairer society.

SOCIAL RANK

The place in society (class) from which you came was of great importance in Edwardian society:

- Mr and Mrs Birling feel that they must, at all costs, retain respectability and social standing.
- Mr Birling, like many manufacturers in the Victorian and Edwardian period, has amassed wealth, which makes him more acceptable to the aristocracy, a class above his, who were often losing money from estates that were costly to maintain.
- We are led to believe that Arthur Birling was not born wealthy, but is a self-made man, keen to keep rising up the social ladder and gain a knighthood (p. 8).
- His knighthood will also make his daughter more acceptable to Lady Croft, Gerald's mother (p. 8).
- Mrs Birling, her husband's 'social superior' (p. 1), has strict manners and behaviour (p. 2).

KEY CONTEXT (A03)

Not all manufacturers held the same views towards the working class as Arthur Birling. Seebohm Rowntree (1871–1954), a chocolate manufacturer, carried out research into poverty. He found that a high percentage of the population lived below the poverty line as a result of low wages – the 'usual rates' (p. 15) that Arthur Birling paid.

TOP TIP (A01)

Remember that, though Gerald genuinely cares for Daisy Renton, he agrees that Mr Birling was right to sack workers like her (pp. 15, 17). You could argue that despite Gerald's sensitivity and kindness, his readiness to take up a mistress from the lower classes and dispense with her when he pleases, is not dissimilar to Mr Birling's dealings with his workers (p. 15).

POLITICAL AND WORKING LIFE IN 1912

In 1912 the Liberal party is in power under the Prime Minister Herbert Henry Asquith and the Labour Party, founded by James Kier Hardie, is beginning to make headway. Suffragettes, calling for votes for women, smash shop windows in London's Oxford Street, and coal miners, after a national strike, secure a minimum wage (meaning pay cannot fall below a particular rate).

- Employers at this time, with the same attitude as Mr Birling (pp. 6, 15) do not take trade unions seriously, though the unions do have more powers to negotiate with the employer than workers who take unorganised action.

- The strike Eva Smith took part in was not led by a trade union, so had little chance of success (p. 15).

- Women are paid less than men for doing the same or a similar job.

- There is no job security for working people like Eva Smith. Dismissal without good references means it is even harder to find work.

- There is no unemployment pay or benefits to help while looking for a new job, so people go hungry, as Eva Smith did (p. 51).

KEY CONTEXT (A03)

Mr Birling scoffs at 'these Bernard Shaws and H. G. Wellses' (p. 7). Both were writers and socialists who commented on inequality and corruption in society. H. G. Wells addressed social class in *The Time Machine* (1895), as did Shaw in his first play, *Widower's Houses* (1892).

KEY QUOTATION: HUNGER (A01)

Priestley's avoids revealing all the details of Eva Smith's life, but when Eric meets her at the Palace Theatre bar he tells us that 'she'd not had much to eat that day' (p. 51). We can assume that a reluctance to make money as a prostitute has left her hungry and poverty stricken and has forced her back to the life she hates at the Palace bar.

TOP TIP: PLACE AND PEOPLE (A03)

Remember that Priestley deliberately chooses a context in which there is a marked divide between the lives of the rich and the poor. In addition to employment, the poor are dependent on the rich for welfare, which may not always be given (for example, the Brumley Women's Charity Organizaton may choose to offer help or not, p. 42). So there are no guarantees that women like Eva Smith (or the 'John Smiths' the Inspector refers to on p. 56) will be able to avoid misery and poverty. Also note that, ironically, one place where the rich and poor meet socially is the Palace Theatre bar. Men like Eric (and possibly Gerald) and local dignitaries, such as Alderman Meggarty (p. 35), gather there to meet prostitutes. Women such as Eva Smith who cannot find legitimate work turn to prostitution to make a living and are dependent on the wealthy yet again, but in a different context.

SETTINGS

The action of the play takes place in a single setting that does not change: the Birlings' dining room one evening in spring, 1912.

- Choosing to set the play in one room only, helps to create a claustrophobic mood.
- The setting is realistic, depicting a normal suburban home, but Priestley will strip away this normality as more and more is revealed about the characters' behaviour towards Eva Smith.
- The lighting is described as 'pink and intimate' (p. 1) when the play opens. This changes to a harsher light when the Inspector arrives, suggesting that his inquiries will be clear sighted and probing.

The Birlings' home is situated in a fictional north Midlands city.

- Brumley is a manufacturing city in which factory owners such as the prosperous Birlings provide employment for the working classes.
- The city has a mayor, aldermen, police force and town hall as well as other institutions. Milwards, the shop mentioned, serves the wealthy.
- The Brumley Women's Charity Organization offers some help to the city's poorer women.
- The Palace Variety Theatre bar is where prostitutes hope to find trade among middle-class men of all ages.

> **KEY CONTEXT** (A03)
>
> The name Brumley has connotations with Birmingham's nickname 'Brum'. Brumley is also onomatopoeic, with a deep, engine-like sound, reminding us of the manufacturing industry that Birmingham was once famous for.

TOP TIP: A REALISTIC SETTING (A03)

Priestley was concerned to present as realistic a stage set as possible, giving detailed and lengthy stage directions at the beginning of Act One. The effect is that of a typical prosperous middle-class dining room of the period, portraying stability, prosperity and convention. The family are dressed in traditional formal evening dress (the men in 'white tie and tails' (p.1) for the celebratory occasion.

The stage directions describe the dining room as 'substantial and comfortable, but not cosy and homelike' (p. 1). The lack of homeliness suggests the hidden tension between the members of the family, which emerges as the play progresses.

MODERN STAGE ADAPTATIONS

Stephen Daldry's adaptation of *An Inspector Calls* (1992–5 and 2009–10) changes Priestley's realistic setting.

- Different time periods are created. The house is set in 1912, but is placed in London during the Second World War. Inspector Goole gives his final speech to the audience in the present day.
- The Edwardian house opens like a flimsy doll's house surrounded by the rubble of the London blitz.
- The lighting creates shadows and pools of light, and the music is menacing.
- A crowd of characters comes on stage, including three children scavenging for food thrown by Edna, the maid.

Do you think Priestley would approve? Think of a reason for each point.

The factory

Milwards

Palace Variety
Theatre

The Birlings' house

The police station

Hospital/mortuary

PROGRESS AND REVISION CHECK

SECTION ONE: CHECK YOUR KNOWLEDGE

Answer these quick questions to test your basic knowledge of the themes, contexts and settings of the play:

1 Which characters learn that they live in an unequal society?

2 Who regards marriage as a means of climbing the social ladder?

3 What twist occurs at the end of the play?

4 Who can be described as a self-made man?

5 Where is the lighting 'pink and intimate'?

6 Name four kinds of love in the play.

7 What is the name of the city in which the play takes place?

8 What type of city is it and where is it?

9 When is the play set?

10 When does the lighting become brighter and harder?

SECTION TWO: CHECK YOUR UNDERSTANDING

Here is a task about the setting of the play. This requires more thought and a slightly longer response. Try to write at least three to four paragraphs.

Task: What effect is Priestley trying to achieve through the setting of the play? Think about:

● What the stage directions and set design tell you

● What they suggest about the characters and their values

PROGRESS CHECK

GOOD PROGRESS

I can:

● explain the main themes, contexts and settings in the text and how they contribute to the effect on the reader. ☐

● use a range of appropriate evidence to support any points I make about these elements. ☐

EXCELLENT PROGRESS

I can:

● analyse in detail the way themes are developed and presented across the play. ☐

● refer closely to key aspects of context and setting and the implications they have for the writer's viewpoint, and the interpretation of relationships and ideas. ☐

PART FIVE: FORM, STRUCTURE AND LANGUAGE

FORM

OVERVIEW

A play's form is its dramatic style. *An Inspector Calls* belongs to more than one type, but it is usually described as a well-made play, a traditional form.

- It has a strong main plot in which events are linked by cause and effect (as we see with Eva Smith's story).
- There is often a revelation about something or someone in which letters or documents are important.
- There is a backstory, in which events have already happened before the play begins.
- Usually, in the traditional well-made play, the conflict is resolved and there is a return to normality. *An Inspector Calls* is different. The twist at the end of the play leaves us asking what will happen next.

THE THREE UNITIES

Priestley wanted the form of his play to be uniform and he followed the three unities:

- unity of action: one main plot that moves on rapidly and smoothly through the play.
- unity of time: the action takes place over a short period in the real time of the play.
- unity of place: the play takes place in a single location (the dining room).

A MORALITY PLAY

An Inspector Calls has been called a morality play, a play with a moral or principle rather like a fable or parable. This dramatic style dates back to the fourteenth and fifteenth centuries. Characters were presented as ideas. So, for example, one character might be 'Justice', another 'Hope' and another 'Pride'. A morality play had religious themes and was concerned with moral behaviour. We can see how Priestley's themes of equality and responsibility are moral ones.

TOP TIP (A02)

There are many different moods in the play, but you can sum up the general pattern from beginning to end: the opening has a *festive* mood until the Inspector arrives, when it changes to *seriousness* and then *anxiety* as the characters are questioned; anxiety turns to *fear* when the Inspector delivers his final monologue, then *relief* when he is discovered to be a fake, only to turn to *shock* at the very end of the play.

TOP TIP: WRITING ABOUT THE FORM OF THE PLAY (A01)

Note how the play shares some of the features of a whodunit or crime drama. When the imposing figure of the Inspector arrives and the lighting becomes 'brighter and harder' (p. 1) we know that the shift in mood means there will be a serious investigation of some kind. The characters are closely interrogated and the play unfolds through the uncovering of clues and information. Priestley borrows these techniques from the whodunit to help create suspense.

STRUCTURE

OVERVIEW

The structure of the play is the way the play is organised. *An Inspector Calls* follows the conventional three acts and has several distinct features.

- The curtain lifts on a celebratory dinner.
- When the Inspector arrives the mood quickly changes and there are revelations involving the characters.
- There is a build up of tension and a climax at the end of Act One and Two followed by a release of tension and further revelations, but the tension and the climax are greater in Act Two.
- Act Three follows a similar pattern to the first two, except that the climax of the play is reached when the Inspector delivers his final monologue.
- There is a release of tension when the Inspector leaves and the remaining characters believe they are finding a resolution (since they believe the visit was some kind of hoax).
- At the very end there is a twist to the denouement (ending) and we are taken back to the beginning of the play.

THE INSPECTOR'S INVOLVEMENT IN THE STRUCTURE

Priestley uses the Inspector to link the 'chain of events' (p. 14) of Eva Smith's story through 'One person and one line of enquiry at a time' (p. 12) and also through the use of the photograph and the diary. The way characters exit or enter allows particular characters to be questioned, or subsequent events to occur that might not have otherwise. For example, Eric's absence from the stage means that tension can be built around his part in the story, so that we suspect his involvement before he tells us about it. Another important example is Gerald's exit (p. 40). By allowing Gerald to leave and return later, Priestley ensures that the exploration of Inspector Goole's identity can take place when the Inspector has left.

EVA SMITH'S JOURNEY

If we assume Eva Smith was one person, we can trace her journey according to the Inspector's investigations and the characters' statements. Priestley has worked out her movements thoroughly over a two-year span and they fit together neatly into this timeline.

- September 1910 she is dismissed form Birling's factory (p. 13).
- December 1910 she begins work at Milwards (p. 20).
- January 1911 she is dismissed from Milwards (pp. 20, 33).
- March 1911 she meets Gerald (p. 34).
- September 1911 her affair with Gerald ends (pp. 38, 43).
- From September to November 1911 she spends time at the seaside (p. 39).
- November 1911 she meets Eric (p. 51).
- Spring 1912 she meets Mrs Birling (p. 43).
- Spring 1912 she commits suicide (p. 11).

TOP TIP: WRITING ABOUT TWISTS IN THE PLAY (A01)

You need to be clear about when the two twists in the play occur and the effects created. The context of the play is realistic from the beginning of the play until the Inspector exits the stage. Priestley introduces us to the first twist when suspicion grows about who Inspector Goole is and Gerald enters with the news, 'That man wasn't a police officer' (p. 62). The effect is that we question the identity of the Inspector and also wonder if we have moved from realism to fantasy. Is the Inspector human at all? The second twist confirms the fantasy element at the end of the play, as the events are about to repeat themselves.

TOP TIP (A01)

Find examples of how Priestley uses stage directions to encourage the actors to build up tension. For instance, when Eric realises that his mother refused Daisy Renton help, the following stage directions come one after the other: 'Mrs B. (alarmed)'; 'Mrs B. (distressed, shakes her head but does not reply)'; 'Eric: (nearly at breaking point)'; 'Mrs B. (very distressed now)'; 'Eric: (almost threatening her)' (pp. 54, 55).

EXAM FOCUS: WRITING ABOUT EFFECTS (A02)

Here is what one student has written about the way Priestley structures events and their effect after the Inspector has left the stage:

> When the Inspector has left, Priestley carefully structures the events. Sheila's comment 'was he really a police inspector?' introduces suspicions about Inspector Goole. The Inspector's case is then logically dismantled, particularly by Gerald, so that not only is the Inspector's identity questioned, but also Eva Smith's. This rational approach has the effect of making the audience feel that the characters will return to the stable situation depicted at the beginning of the play, just like an ordinary resolution in a narrative. Consequently, the final phone call as the twist at the end of the play comes as an even greater shock than it might have.

Quotation embedded in the text

Comparison is useful to support a point

Shows the effect on the audience

Conjunctive adverb linking cause and effect

Now you try it:

Add a final sentence contrasting the logical approach described and the ending of the play.

LANGUAGE

OVERVIEW

- J. B. Priestley's writing in *An Inspector Calls* has great energy and directness. We can be in no doubt about the main character's convictions. Inspector Goole is an impassioned **orator** and the effect on the audience is to regard his words as Priestley's views.

- There are few **metaphors** or **similes** in the play. Priestley prefers to use natural speech as spoken by the middle and upper classes of the time.

- Some expressions, such as 'squiffy' (p. 3), seem archaic to our ears. Nevertheless, they help to convey a character's nature and give us a sense of the Edwardian period.

J. B. Priestley

LANGUAGE DEVICE: VOICE

What is **voice**?	The way a character speaks or the distinctive manner in which the playwright addresses the audience.
Example	When Mr and Mrs Birling and Eric are quarrelling heatedly the Inspector takes charge *'masterfully'* calling 'Stop!' and the other characters *'are suddenly quiet, staring at him'*.
Effect	It portrays the Inspector's ability to exert power and control, and also how the other characters seem compelled to listen, as though under a spell.

TOP TIP (A02)

Remember that when you comment on Priestley's dialogue and use of different literary techniques, such as irony, euphemism, symbolism, rhetoric and so on, you should always discuss the *effect* that they create on the audience.

Priestley's dialogue portrays a broad range of traits so that all the **characters** have distinctive personalities: the moody and explosive Eric, the tight-lipped Sybil Birling and the discreet Gerald. Arthur Birling and Sheila share the Inspector's directness, even bluntness in the case of Arthur Birling, who is also given to oratory, but of a different kind. In Act One, before the Inspector arrives, Mr Birling delivers several speeches. The other characters are obliged to listen, particularly Eric, as his father's dialogue is peppered with 'I hope Eric' (p. 4) or 'Just let me finish, Eric. You've got a lot to learn' (p. 6). The effect is that we are immediately aware of Mr Birling's pompous and self-righteous nature and the strained relationship between father and son.

Priestley's **stage directions** give us an idea of how he sees his characters. He tells us that Mr Birling is *'rather provincial in his speech'* (p. 2), which conveys a lack of sophistication and refinement. Sheila is *'rather excited'* (p. 2), which is borne out in her lively exchange at the dinner table, and Eric is *'half shy, half assertive'* (p. 1), which is shown in his badly timed exclamations or interruptions: *'Eric suddenly guffaws'* (p. 3).

LANGUAGE DEVICE: IRONY

What is irony?	Expressions or situations that may suggest something different from the obvious meaning.
Example	When Sheila reproaches Gerald for neglecting her the previous summer he dismisses her concerns and she retorts playfully, 'that's what *you* say' (p. 3).
Effect	Sheila does not know that Gerald had been having an affair with Daisy Renton. At the time Sheila makes her remark we wonder if Sheila is being deceived. We find out later that she is.

Irony is the device most often used in *An Inspector Calls*. This is not surprising since Inspector Goole's purpose is to expose the double standards people such as the Birlings practise. The play's focus is the constant uncovering of each character's guilt, secrets or lies. The most shocking dramatic irony is Mrs Birling's persistent condemnation of the father of Eva Smith's unborn child, before she grasps that it is her own son, and the baby, had it been born, her own grandchild (pp. 48–9).

Looking at the play as a whole, we could say that the overarching irony is Mr Birling's complete faith in his way of life and the idea of progress, as if life could only get better, when two years later the country will be at war. If we think that Priestley is addressing the audience as well as the characters, what is the effect? Are we in a position to judge the Birlings? How far do we behave responsibly towards others and help to create a just community, or do we only care about ourselves?

LANGUAGE DEVICE: EUPHEMISM

What is euphemism?	A word or phrase that is mild and less blunt than the actual subject.
Example	Mrs Birling refers to 'a girl of that sort' (p. 47).
Effect	We know that she really means a young woman who has few morals.

Being well mannered was important in the Edwardian period and the use of euphemism in the play should be seen in this context, where it is mainly used to refer to any sexual matters in order not to shock the female characters. There is also a contrast between the way different characters speak and observe accepted codes of behaviour. Mr Birling's manner is far less sophisticated than Gerald's. For example, when Mr Birling raises the question of Lady Croft's approval of Sheila he says bluntly what he believes Lady Croft thinks: that Gerald 'might have done better … socially'. Gerald 'embarrassed' glosses over the comment (p. 8). It is an issue that Gerald would never raise because it would be considered impolite or distasteful.

TOP TIP (A02)

Turn to this example of the use of language in the conversation between Mrs Birling and the Inspector, where she asks if he will 'take offence' (p. 31) meaning would he be insulted. But 'offence' has a double meaning and refers to the noun meaning a 'crime' as well. The irony exists for us in hindsight when we discover the crime Mrs Birling committed against Eva Smith and her unborn child.

TOP TIP (A01)

Note the use of slang such as 'Chump!' (p. 5) and 'goggle-eyed' (p. 35) and who uses it. Who disapproves of slang? What does their language tell you about the characters and/or their different generations?

LANGUAGE DEVICE: SYMBOLISM

What is symbolism?	When an object or person represents something else, usually an idea or quality.
Example	Eva Smith and Edna the parlour maid stand for those who have little or no power over their own lives.
Effect	The fact that Eva Smith is unable to halt her decline into poverty because she is at the mercy of those more powerful than herself creates a sense of the failure of society in its duties.

Most of the characters are symbols of particular social types. The Inspector is the truth seeker. Sheila and Eric are the younger generation whose views are as yet undeveloped. Mr and Mrs Birling, the older generation, are fixed and rigid in their views. Gerald symbolises the young upper-class gentleman – sophisticated and stylish.

LANGUAGE DEVICE: IMAGE

What is an image?	It creates a word picture; common forms are metaphors and similes.
Example	Mr Birling says, 'as if we were all mixed up together like bees in a hive – community and all that nonsense' (p. 10).
Effect	This simile compares the image of a hive of bees with people of all kinds mixed together as part of a community. Mr Birling sneers at this idea.

The most important metaphor Priestley creates is 'fire and blood and anguish' (p. 56). Spoken by the Inspector in his final speech and repeated by Sheila (p. 71) it represents a breakdown in society, whether as war, revolution or another horror. The characters and the audience feel its impact since the metaphor is part of a rhetorical monologue meant to arrest our attention.

TOP TIP (A01)

Find details that help you to build images of Gerald. For example, what image do you have of Gerald from this description: 'rather too manly to be a dandy' (p. 1) and his comment 'I'm rather more – upset – by this business than I probably appear to be' (p. 39)?

LANGUAGE DEVICE: RHETORIC

What is rhetoric?	It is the technique of using language to persuade or convince others.
Example	Inspector Goole says, 'This girl killed herself – and died a horrible death. But each of you helped to kill her. Remember that. Never forget it.' (p. 55)
Effect	The effect is to make the characters and audience pay attention to the seriousness of the point being made.

Note how Priestley uses long and short sentences in quick succession to give impact through a sharp change of pace. A long sentence is followed by his final abrupt words to the Birlings, 'Good night', before he leaves the stage.

PROGRESS AND REVISION CHECK

SECTION ONE: CHECK YOUR KNOWLEDGE

Answer these quick questions to test your basic knowledge of the form, structure and language of the play:

1. What do we call the way a character speaks?
2. What do we call a milder word or phrase in place of a more blunt one?
3. What style of speaking does the Inspector use to convince others?
4. What is a religious play with a moral called?
5. What do we call the linked episodes of Eva Smith's story?
6. What word do we use for a play's dramatic style?
7. What name do we give to the way a play is organised?
8. What is the name for events that have happened before the play begins?
9. What is a lengthy speech by one person called?
10. What do we call a character's distinctive quality?

SECTION TWO: CHECK YOUR UNDERSTANDING

Here is a task about the form of the play. This requires more thought and a slightly longer response. Try to write at least three to four paragraphs.

Task: What are the features of a well-made play as a traditional form?
Think about:

- The features of a whodunit or crime drama
- How *An Inspector Calls* fits a whodunit, but is also different at the end

PROGRESS CHECK

GOOD PROGRESS

I can:

- explain how Priestley uses form, structure and language to develop the action, show relationships and develop ideas. ☐
- use relevant quotations to support the points I make, and make reference to the effect of some language choices. ☐

EXCELLENT PROGRESS

I can:

- analyse in detail Priestley's use of particular forms, structures and language techniques to convey ideas, create characters and evoke mood or setting. ☐
- select from a range of evidence, including apt quotations, to infer the effect of particular language choices and to develop wider interpretations. ☐

PART SIX: PROGRESS BOOSTER

UNDERSTANDING THE QUESTION

For your exam, you will be answering a question on the whole text and/or a question on an extract from *An Inspector Calls*. Check with your teacher to see what sort of question you are doing. Whatever the task, questions in exams will need **decoding**. This means highlighting and understanding the key words so the answer you write is relevant.

TOP TIP (A01)

You might also be asked to 'refer closely to', which means picking out specific examples from the text, or to focus on 'methods and techniques', which means the 'things' Priestley does, for example, the use of a particular dramatic device, a change of mood, etc.

BREAK DOWN THE QUESTION

Pick out the **key words** or phrases. For example:

Question: How does J. B. Priestley **present attitudes** to ambition in *An Inspector Calls?*

Write about:

● Attitudes towards ambition in *An Inspector Calls*
● How Priestley presents these attitudes by the way he writes

What does this tell you?

● Focus on **the theme of ambition** but also on **'attitudes'** – so **different characters'** views on it.
● The word **'present'** tells you that you should focus on the ways Priestley reveals these attitudes, i.e. the techniques he uses.

PLANNING YOUR ANSWER

It is vital that you generate ideas quickly and plan your answer efficiently when you sit the exam. Stick to your plan and, with a watch at your side, tick off each part as you progress.

STAGE 1: GENERATE IDEAS QUICKLY

Very briefly **list your key ideas** based on the question you have **decoded**. For example:

● *Mr Birling's driving ambition*
● *Eric's lack of ambition*
● *Gerald's attitude to ambition*

STAGE 2: JOT DOWN USEFUL QUOTATIONS (OR KEY EVENTS)

For example:

- 'I might find my way into the next Honours List' (p. 8)
- Mr Birling to Eric: 'Apparently nothing matters to you' (p. 57)

STAGE 3: PLAN FOR PARAGRAPHS

Use paragraphs to plan your answer. For example:

Paragraph	Point
Paragraph 1:	**Introduce** the **argument** you wish to make: *Priestley explores the theme of ambition in a variety of ways, mainly through Arthur Birling but also through other characters.*
Paragraph 2:	Your first point: *Arthur Birling has a driving ambition to increase his wealth and status. In particular he wants to achieve a knighthood by whatever means.*
Paragraph 3:	Your second point: *Eric has low self-esteem and seems to lack ambition. He seems to have no interest in his father's firm, perhaps because of his poor relationship with his father, who rarely listens to him. We can assume that before the Inspector's visit at least, Eric would rather spend time drinking or seeking entertainment as a distraction from his anxieties.*
Paragraph 4:	Your third point: *Although Gerald Croft agrees with Mr Birling's business views, he does not seem to share his intense ambition. However, he does seem happy to see the Croft and Birling companies unite.*
Paragraph 5:	Your fourth point: *Mrs Birling is keen to maintain or improve her social status and therefore we assume she is ambitious to see Sheila marry Gerald, since he is the son of a lord.*
Paragraph 6:	Your fifth point: *At the beginning of the play Sheila seems keen to marry Gerald because she loves him, but like most middle-class Edwardian young women we can assume she wants to marry 'well'.*
Conclusion:	**Sum up** your argument: *Finally, we could argue that Priestley presents Inspector Goole as ambitious, not for himself, but he is determined to see the wrongs done to Eva Smith put right, so that justice is done.*

TOP TIP (A02)

When discussing Priestley's language, make sure you refer to the techniques he uses and, most importantly, the *effect* of those techniques. Don't just say, 'Priestley uses the dash a lot', write, 'When Priestley uses the dash to show that Eric is angry, the break in the dialogue demonstrates Eric's faltering sentences.'

RESPONDING TO WRITERS' EFFECTS

The two most important assessment objectives are **AO1** and **AO2**. They are about *what* writers do (the choices they make, and the effects these create), *what* your ideas are (your analysis and interpretation) and *how* you write about them (how well you explain your ideas).

ASSESSMENT OBJECTIVE 1

What does it say?	What does it mean?	Dos and Don'ts
Read, understand and respond to texts. Students should be able to: • Maintain a critical style and develop an informed personal response • Use textual references, including quotations, to support and illustrate interpretations	You must: • Use some of the literary terms you have learned (correctly!) • Write in a professional way (not a sloppy, chatty way) • Show that you have thought for yourself • Back up your ideas with examples, including quotations	**Don't write …** *Gerald tells Mrs Birling 'apologetically' that Eric drinks. So that tells us he is unhappy.* **Do write …** *Priestley presents Eric as a troubled young person. The stage directions tell us that Gerald confirms 'apologetically' to Mrs Birling that Eric drinks. The adverb 'apologetically' suggests that Gerald is aware that Eric's drinking is a social embarrassment.*

IMPROVING YOUR CRITICAL STYLE

Use a variety of words to show effects:

Priestley *suggests …, conveys …, implies …, presents …, explores …, demonstrates …, describes how …, shows how …*

I/we (as readers) *infer …, recognise …, understand …, question …, see …, are given …, reflect …*

For example, look at these two alternative paragraphs by different students about Gerald Croft. Note the difference in the quality of expression:

Student A:

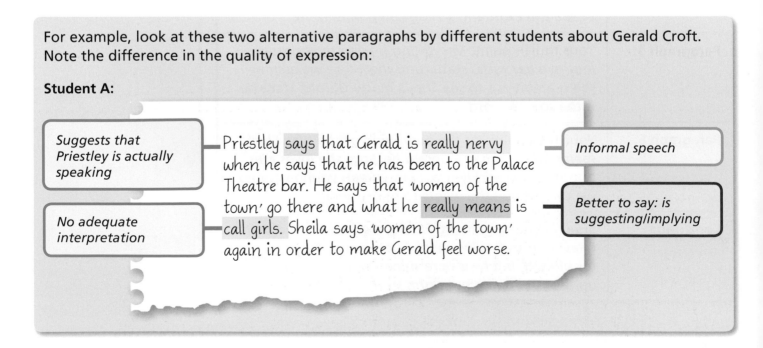

Suggests that Priestley is actually speaking

No adequate interpretation

Priestley says that Gerald is really nervy when he says that he has been to the Palace Theatre bar. He says that 'women of the town' go there and what he really means is call girls. Sheila says 'women of the town' again in order to make Gerald feel worse.

Informal speech

Better to say: is suggesting/implying

Student B:

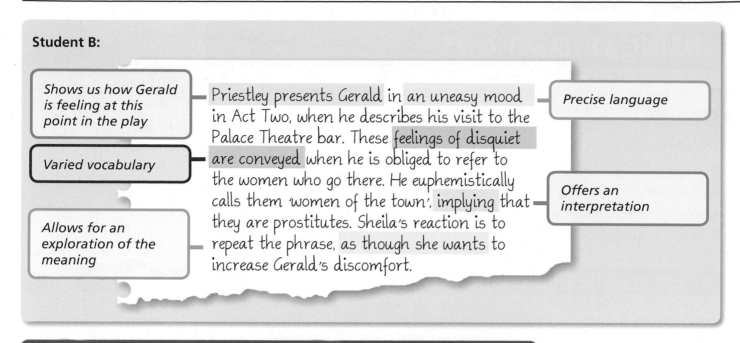

Shows us how Gerald is feeling at this point in the play

Varied vocabulary

Allows for an exploration of the meaning

Priestley presents Gerald in an uneasy mood in Act Two, when he describes his visit to the Palace Theatre bar. These feelings of disquiet are conveyed when he is obliged to refer to the women who go there. He euphemistically calls them 'women of the town', implying that they are prostitutes. Sheila's reaction is to repeat the phrase, as though she wants to increase Gerald's discomfort.

Precise language

Offers an interpretation

ASSESSMENT OBJECTIVE 2

What does it say?	What does it mean?	Dos and Don'ts
Analyse the language, form and structure used by the writer to create meanings and effects, using relevant subject terminology where appropriate.	'Analyse' – comment **in detail** on **particular aspects** of the text or language. 'Language' – vocabulary, imagery, variety of sentences, dialogue/speech etc. 'Form' – **how** the story is told (e.g. comedy, tragedy, crime drama, morality play, act, scene) 'Structure'– the **order** in which events are revealed, or in which characters appear, or in which **climaxes** occur 'create meaning' – what can we, as readers, **infer** from what the writer tells us? What is **implied** by particular descriptions, or events? 'Subject terminology' – **words** you should use when **writing** about plays, such as 'character', 'dialogue', 'stage directions', etc.	**Don't write …** *Sheila is rude to Gerald so I know she is angry with him.* **Do write …** *Priestley conveys Sheila's anger with Gerald when she uses the* **metaphor** *'Fairy Prince' to describe his behaviour with Daisy Renton. The metaphor* **suggests** *both a gallant hero who comes to the rescue and the element of fantasy,* **implying** *the affair could not last.*

THE THREE 'I'S

- The best analysis focuses on specific ideas or events, or uses of language and thinks about what is **implied**.
- This means drawing **inferences**. Sheila's description of Gerald shows us how angry and hurt she must feel about his affair, but what deeper meanings does it convey if, for example she can use sarcasm? What does it suggest about their relationship, and whether or not it can last?
- From the inferences you make across the text as a whole, you can arrive at your own **interpretation** – a sense of the bigger picture, a wider evaluation of a person, relationship or idea.

USING QUOTATIONS

One of the secrets of success in writing exam essays is to use quotations **effectively**. There are five basic principles:

1. Only quote what is most useful.
2. Do not use a quotation that repeats what you have just written.
3. Put quotation marks, e.g. ' ', around the quotation.
4. Write the quotation exactly as it appears in the original.
5. Use the quotation so that it fits neatly into your sentence.

EXAM FOCUS: USING QUOTATIONS

Quotations should be used to develop the line of thought in your essay and to 'zoom in' on key details such as language choices. The example below shows a clear and effective way of doing this:

> **Gives an apt quotation**
>
> Priestley presents Gerald as an upper-class young man and describes him as 'rather too manly to be a dandy'. The mention of the word 'dandy' does suggest that Gerald has some vanity about him, even though Priestley describes him as not quite a 'dandy'.
>
> **Makes a clear point**
>
> **Explains the effect of the quotation**

However, really **high-level responses** will go further. They will make an even more precise point, support it with an even more appropriate quotation, focus in on particular words and phrases and explain the effect or what is implied to make a wider point or draw inferences. Here is an example:

> **Apt quotation**
>
> **Explains the effect of language**
>
> In the stage directions Priestley presents Gerald as upper class, young and easy going and adds that he is 'rather too manly to be a dandy', a more revealing description. The noun 'dandy' implies vanity. Despite Gerald not being quite a dandy, there is a suggestion that vanity is part of his nature – which may have been a factor in his rescue of Daisy Renton at the Palace bar.
>
> **Opens with a precise point**
>
> **Refers to a specific word**
>
> **Draws inferences to make a wider point about the character**

SPELLING, PUNCTUATION AND GRAMMAR

SPELLING

Remember to spell correctly the **author's** name, the names of all the **characters**, and the names of **places**.

It is a good idea to list some of the key spellings you know you sometimes get wrong *before* the exam starts. Then use it to check as you go along. Sometimes it is easy to make small errors as you write, but if you have your key word list nearby you can check against it.

PUNCTUATION

Remember:

- Use **full stops and commas in sentences accurately to make clear points**. Don't write long, rambling sentences that don't make sense; equally, avoid using a lot of short repetitive ones. Write in a fluent way, using linking words and phrases and use **inverted commas** for **quotations**:

Don't write	Do write
When Inspector Goole arrives there is a shift of mood, the stage lighting changes from soft to harsh, the inspector stands squarely, he gives the impression that he has an important job to do, and he speaks weightily.	*When Inspector Goole arrives there is a shift of mood **as** the light changes from soft to harsh. The inspector stands squarely, **giving** the impression that he has an important job to do. His imposing presence is added to by the 'weightily' tone of his speech.*

GRAMMAR

When you are writing about the text, make sure you:

- Use the present tense for discussing what the writer does.
- Use pronouns and references back to make your writing flow.

Don't write	Do write
Although Eric seemed to be an apathetic, unhappy young man, Eric's view of the world seems to change for the better as Eric questioned his actions after the Inspector's visit.	*Although Eric **seems** to be an apathetic, unhappy young man, **his** view of the world seems to change for the better as **he questions** his actions after the Inspector's visit.*

TOP TIP A04

Remember that spelling, punctuation and grammar is worth **approximately 5%** of your overall marks, which could mean the difference between one grade and another.

TOP TIP A04

Practise the spellings of key literary terms you might use when writing about the text such as: irony, euphemism, simile, metaphor, imagery, protagonist, character, theme, climax, etc.

TOP TIP A04

Enliven your essay by varying the way your sentences begin. For example, *Mrs Birling is forced to answer the Inspector's question, despite her reluctance to do so,* can also be written as: *Despite her reluctance to do so, Mrs Birling is forced to answer the Inspector's questions.*

ANNOTATED SAMPLE ANSWERS

This section will provide you with three **sample responses**, to give you an idea of what is required to **achieve** at different levels.

> **Question:** How does Mrs Birling respond to the Inspector's visit?
>
> Write about:
> - How Priestley presents the character of Mrs Birling
> - Why she responds in the way she does

SAMPLE ANSWER 1

A01 Introduces the main basic characteristics of Mrs Birling

J. B. Priestley presents Sybil Birling as a very cold woman and this is because she thinks she is better than anyone else. She thinks she is an important person, like Mr Birling does.

A01 New point signalled in new paragraph

In Act two she tries to bully Sheila telling her to go to bed and then she starts to tell Inspector Goole off. She tells him all about Mr Birling being a mayor and a magistrate. She says, 'You know of course that my husband was Lord Mayor only two years ago', but the Inspector takes no notice.

A03 Reference to the context in which the play is set

Sybil Birling does not care about other people. She does not want to help poor people if she thinks they haven't earned it. For example, she says to the Inspector, 'we've been helping deserving cases'. This means she doesn't want to help people she doesn't think deserve it. In those days people had to rely on charities because there were no benefits from the government. When Eva Smith really needed help from her charity, because she was expecting a baby, Sybil Birling wouldn't give it because she didn't like Eva Smith. This was because Eva Smith called herself Mrs Birling. Sybil Birling was cross because she thought it was rude. She says, 'I think it was simply a piece of gross impertinence'. What she didn't know was that Eva Smith had a right to call herself that because Eric Birling was the father of her baby. On top of that Sybil says to the Inspector that he ought to be looking for who the father is and when he finds him, punish him. But, as I said, Sybil doesn't know Eric is the father.

A02 A clear detailed explanation given, but the literary device (irony) not highlighted

A01 Informal expression unsuitable – should use a critical style

All Sybil Birling cares about is keeping up appearances. She doesn't want the Inspector to find out any nasty secrets, so she wants him to go away. Everything was going well for her, she was having a little engagement party for Sheila and Gerald and they were enjoying themselves, she was very pleased about the engagement because Gerald's father is Lord Croft. This means Sheila would get to be Lady Croft at some point and that would just suit Sybil Birling.

A04 Sentence too long – there are several sentences contained in one; also includes irrelevant details

There are some nasty parts in the play. One is where Sheila tells her mother that her brother Eric drinks too much. Sybil Birling doesn't believe her and in a way Sheila shouldn't have said anything because later in the play, Sybil Birling says to Eric 'you're not the type – you don't get drunk'. So it shows she can't face the truth.

A01 A quotation but not fully embedded

A02 An explanation of the effect, but expressed rather clumsily

Another nasty part is when Eric blames his mother for killing Eva Smith and her grandchild, the one that wasn't born. He is very angry and Sybil Birling gets upset and says she didn't know that he was the father when Eva Smith came to ask for help. Eric more or less says his mother never understands anything and that she doesn't really care about him.

A01 Needs to draw together the main points or find an interesting way to sum up

After this you would think she would be upset for a long time, but she seems to get over it. When she finds out that Inspector Goole may not be a real police inspector, she's back to normal. It shows how cold Sybil Birling is and doesn't seem to be affected by anything deep down.

MID LEVEL

Comment
There is an understanding of the character expressed and some sound points are made. Paragraphs are used effectively, but vocabulary is limited and words or expressions repeated. The overall effect is too chatty in tone. The student needs to write in a more formal style and should also discuss the effects Priestley creates, referring to literary devices.

For a Good Level:
- Develop a formal critical style, drawing on a wider range of vocabulary and avoid informal language or slang.
- Use literary devices and show how the playwright creates effects from the language he chooses.
- Make sure quotations are embedded in sentences so that when a sentence is read it flows easily and the quotation feels part of it.

SAMPLE ANSWER 2

A01 Clear introduction that outlines the essential points

Priestley presents Sybil Birling as a snobbish and unkind woman. She feels herself to be above other people who are not in the same class as she is, and when the Inspector arrives she treats him like an inferior.

She does not meet the Inspector until Act Two. In the meantime he has been questioning other characters and there has been an argument between Sheila and Gerald. When Mrs Birling comes on to the stage she is not prepared for this. Her mood is 'quite out of key' and she does not pick up on the atmosphere and the effect is to make her seem like a busybody. Sheila uses the metaphor 'not to build a wall'. She is trying to tell her mother not to stop the Inspector's inquiries, but Sybil Birling does not understand and she is annoyed. She is also rude to the Inspector, saying that his comments are 'a trifle impertinent'. The word 'impertinent' shows how her attitude to others is a superior one.

A01 A quotation that is embedded fluently in the sentence

A02 Explains the effect of a quotation

Priestley also presents Sybil Birling as someone who does not care how people from the lower classes live. Priestley sees this as part of the problem with the rich in Edwardian times and since there is no government assistance charities need to help. Although Sybil Birling belongs to the Brumley Women's Charity Organization, she only helps those who she thinks have earned it. So when Eva Smith, who is pregnant, asks for help and calls herself Mrs Birling, Sybil Birling is extremely angry and tells her committee not to assist. This is an example of irony, because Sybil Birling doesn't know that Eric is the unborn baby's father. To make things worse, she then tells the Inspector when he is questioning her that the father of the child should be made to pay and be, 'dealt with very severely'.

A03 Reference to the context of the play and point extended

A02 Highlights a literary device and shows its relevance

A04 Shifts successfully to a new paragraph

Sybil Birling does not understand why her daughter Sheila is so impressed with the Inspector. She does not grasp the Inspector's message 'that we are all responsible for one another' and most of the time she goes along with what her husband says. She is more concerned to keep things under wraps and make sure there is no gossip that could harm her family. She is not interested in people outside her own class.

A01 Informal expression – should use critical style

Priestley shows us two points in the play where Sybil Birling's coldness turns to horror. At the end of Act Two there is a climax. This is because she has just realized that Eric is the father of Eva Smith's unborn baby. Although she shouts, 'I won't believe it' we feel she does. The stress on 'won't' means that she doesn't want to believe it. The other point is when Eric gets to find out about his mother refusing help to Eva Smith and he says, 'you killed her – and your own grandchild'. This is a real shock for his mother and she is 'very distressed'. Eric is so angry he is almost violent towards her and the audience must feel the shock too.

A02 Explains the effect by highlighting the key word

You might think Mrs Birling would think hard about what she has done and Eric's problems, but when she speaks next she just blames Eric. She is more concerned with avoiding a scandal, and this tell us that despite everything that has happened she is not willing to learn from the Inspector and change.

A02 A sound conclusion

GOOD LEVEL

Comment
This is a confident response to the question and demonstrates a good understanding of the character's nature and motivations. The context of the play has also been mentioned. Literary devices have been highlighted and there is some exploration of language to emphasise effects. Quotations are relevant and fluently embedded in sentences, but occasionally the language is a little informal.

For a High Level:
- Refer more to Priestley's control of language and purpose.
- Extend the range of vocabulary, and look for more sophisticated words to express ideas.
- Be careful not to use informal language, but to develop a critical style.
- Use long and short sentences to vary pace, and alter sentence openers for variety.

SAMPLE ANSWER 3

A01 Excellent opening that presents the character's importance in the text

Sybil Birling's aloof and contemptuous nature springs from feelings of social superiority and her character (along with her husband's) is central to an understanding of the play. They symbolise everything that Priestley believes is wrong with the Edwardian ruling class: their individualism, their lack of responsibility to the community and their callousness.

A03 Follows on using a literary device to state the author's purpose, linking the text with the context in which it is written

A02 Quotation clearly embedded in the text with interpretation of language and effect

Having been off stage since the celebratory dinner, Mrs Birling is unaware of the dramatic events that have taken place between Sheila and Gerald in the Inspector's presence. In Act Two she bustles in 'briskly and self-confidently, quite out of key' with what has happened. Priestley's stage directions sum up her complete failure to sense the mood. Sheila's attempts to prevent her mother 'building a wall' against the Inspector – a metaphor for resistance – are met with bewilderment and annoyance. Inspector Goole's plain speaking is met with an accusation of impertinence.

Sybil Birling is ignorant of how others, less fortunate, struggle, at a time when there was no welfare state. Her myopic view of the world prevents her from grasping that Eva Smith, whose suicide is the focus of the Inspector's call, visited The Brumley Women's Charity Organization in desperation. The pregnant young woman's offence was to call herself 'Mrs Birling', another apparent impertinence and an irony lost on Sybil. She is unaware that her son Eric was the father of Eva's unborn child. For Sybil, Eva Smith is one of the undeserving poor, so she cruelly uses her influence to refuse charity. Not only that, she takes the opportunity to tell the Inspector in no uncertain terms that the father should be held 'entirely responsible' and 'dealt with very severely'. Another irony.

A04 Precise, well-chosen vocabulary to describe the character

A02 Literary device and its effect highlighted

A02 Sharp effective use of language to reinforce an earlier example of literary device

At the heart of Sybil Birling's character and the reason why the Inspector is so unwelcome is her acute sense of propriety, respectability and status. Maintaining her family's social standing without regard to the needs of the wider society is where she feels her duty lies. She is quite unable to understand Sheila's attitude as her daughter tries to face the crux of the Inspector's (and Priestley's) rhetorical message; that social justice is crucial to society and that without it there will be 'fire and blood and anguish'. For Sybil Birling

A02 Clear, extended analysis links the character to the chief metaphor of the play

anything troubling or unsavoury must be kept hidden. Much of her dialogue is peppered with warnings: 'Careful what you say, dear!' 'Sheila!' 'Arthur!' 'Eric!' The frequency of exclamation marks in her speech reveals anxiety as well as disapproval. Any whiff of scandal alerts her to danger, so she resists the Inspector's interrogation until it is impossible to do so.

A02
Highlights effect of punctuation

There are two occasions in the play where her chilly exterior crumples. The first is the climax of Act Two. We witness her 'frightened glance', as she realises that Eric is the father of the unborn child, leaving us to speculate on what scenes will follow in Act Three. The second occasion is when Eric, 'nearly at breaking point', damns her for killing 'her own grandchild'. The audience is gripped as Sybil pleads that she didn't understand that it was his child, and we see how this lack of understanding is part of her relationship with Eric. He accuses her of never having 'tried' to understand him. We do not know how she reacts to this. She says no more, and only speaks a few pages later to declare her shame at his behaviour. Is this an indication of her heartlessness or her inability to recognise her part in his unhappy life and alcoholism? Certainly, her recovery is remarkable once she thinks the Inspector is a hoax. All the previous revelations have been shuffled away in order to 'behave sensibly'. For Sybil Birling the Inspector's visit brings no epiphany, and we can only assume that she remains unchanged by all that has happened. Or does she? The Inspector, whether a man of insight or a mysterious prophet, warns her that she will 'spend the rest of [her] life regretting' what she did.

A01
Important connection to another part of the play

A04
Excellent use of sentence structure for style and effect

A01
Excellent conclusion challenging assumptions to show a complexity of character

VERY HIGH LEVEL

Comment
This is an excellent critique of Sybil Birling and her motives. There is good use of literary techniques, sound analysis of language and its effect. Links have been made to other features of the play, particularly to the central theme of responsibility and also to the playwright's main purpose. A sophisticated range of vocabulary appropriate to the character has been used and sentence structure has pace and variety. The conclusion presents an unusual and well-supported argument about an aspect of the character.

PRACTICE TASK

Write a full-length response to this exam-style question and then use the **Mark scheme** on page 88 to assess your own response.

> **Question:** How does J. B. Priestley explore love in *An Inspector Calls*?
>
> Write about:
>
> - The ideas about love in *An Inspector Calls*
> - How Priestley presents ideas about love by the ways he writes

TOP TIP (A01)

You can use the General skills section of the **Mark scheme** on page 88 to remind you of the key criteria you'll need to cover.

Remember:

- Plan quickly and efficiently by using key words from the question.
- Focus on the techniques Priestley uses and the effect of these on the reader.
- Support your ideas with relevant evidence, including quotations.

FURTHER QUESTIONS

1 How does J. B. Priestley present the ending of *An Inspector Calls*?

Write about:

- the characters' attitudes at the end of the play
- how Priestley affects the audience by the ways he writes.

2 **Eric Birling:** 'I do take some interest in it. I take too much, that's my trouble.' Explore how Eric's experiences have affected him. You **must** refer to other characters in your answer.

3 Answer both parts of this question:

(a) Read the extract below.

> **Sheila:** Yes, and it was I who had the girl turned out of her job at Milwards. *And* I'm supposed to be engaged to Gerald. And I'm not a child, don't forget. I've a right to know. *Were* you in love with her Gerald?

Look at the way Sheila speaks and behaves in this extract. How may this affect an audience's attitude towards her? Refer closely to details from the extract to support your answer.

(b) What do you think of the character of Edna and the way she is presented in *An Inspector Calls*?

LITERARY TERMS

backstory	events that have happened before the play begins
characters	either a person in a play or novel, or his or her personality
character trait	a distinctive quality of a character that often makes them different from other characters
climax	the highpoint of a play or act.
coup de théâtre	a sudden and spectacular turn of events in the plot of a play
dialogue	speech and conversation between characters
dramatic irony	occurs when the development of the plot allows the audience to know more about what is happening than some of the characters do
euphemism	unpleasant, embarrassing or frightening facts or words can be concealed behind a 'euphemism' – a word or phrase less blunt or offensive
homophone	two or more words that have the same pronunciation, but different origins, meanings and sometimes spellings (e.g. 'pair' and 'pear')
imagery	creating a word picture; common forms are metaphors and similes
irony	saying one thing while meaning another, often through understatement, concealment or indirect statement
literary technique	methods used by authors to create effects and meaning. Also called a literary device
metaphor	a figure of speech in which something, someone or an action is described as something else in order to imply a resemblance
monologue	lengthy speech by one person
oratory	the dignified, formal style used by someone making a speech in a public place
polemic	a piece of writing expressing an argument about important social issues such as religion or politics
protagonist	the central character of the play or narrative
rhetoric	a technique for using language effectively to convince or persuade
rhetorical	fluent in using language effectively to convince or persuade
sarcasm	an extreme form of irony, usually intended to be hurtful
simile	a figure of speech using 'like' or 'as' to make a comparison
stage directions	advice printed in the text of a play giving instructions or information about the movements, gestures and appearance of the actors, or on the setting or special effects required at a particular moment in the action
symbolism	use of an object or person to represent something else, possibly an idea or quality
theme	a central idea examined by an author
the three unities	in Classical Greek drama, plays conformed to the unities of action, time and place – one complete action happening in a single day or night. The unity of place was added later and was usually in one location.
voice	a character's speech or the distinctive way the playwright addresses the audience.
well-made play	a play that exhibits a neatness of plot and smooth-functioning exactness of action, with all its parts fitting together precisely. *An Inspector Calls* works through an interlocking series of unexpected discourses, leading to a final revelation that is almost a trick ending
whodunit	a novel, play etc. concerned with crime, usually a murder

CHECKPOINT ANSWERS

CHECKPOINT 1, page 11

- Mr Birling is a self-important man.
- He has a strong belief in his own position of power.
- He wants to be accepted into society and is proud of his humble start in life.
- He has a narrow view of the world.
- He prefers to believe what suits his purpose.

CHECKPOINT 2, page 14

- The Inspector uses the expression a 'chain of events' (Act One, p. 14) quite early on.
- The Inspector's method of questioning each member of the family in turn adds to this sense of there being a chain.
- The deliberate mention of the time of each event links what one character has done to what the next one questioned has done.
- There are aspects of the girl's description, manner and behaviour that are common to more than one character's memory of her.
- Mr Birling's sacking of Eva Smith makes him the first link in the chain.

CHECKPOINT 3, page 17

- Eva Smith died in the Infirmary after swallowing disinfectant.
- She had left a letter, a photograph and a diary.
- She had used more than one name.
- She had been employed in Mr Birling's factory and was sacked in September 1910 for asking for higher wages.
- Both her parents were dead.
- She had been out of work for two months, had no savings and was becoming desperate.
- She had got a job at Milwards but had been sacked in January 1911 after a customer complained about her.
- She had changed her name to Daisy Renton and had decided to try another kind of life.

CHECKPOINT 4, page 19

- The Inspector decides who will be questioned and when.
- He decides who will or will not see the photograph.
- He makes Mr Birling recognise the implications of the possibility of others being involved in the 'chain of events' (Act One, p. 14).
- He contradicts Birling and overrules his wish that Sheila should leave the room.
- His method of questioning draws confessions from Mr Birling and Sheila.
- He makes it clear he will not leave until he knows 'all that happened' (Act One, p. 25).
- His catches out Gerald by dropping in the name of Daisy Renton.

CHECKPOINT 5, page 24

Mr Birling:

- is reluctant to discuss his business
- refuses to see that he has done wrong
- is unmoved by the girl's death
- has little concern for what might have happened to the girl after he sacked her
- is casual about the idea that the girl may have had to 'Go on the streets' (Act One, p. 16)
- is concerned only about his business and his profits.

Gerald:

- tells the story fully, after a brief attempt at denying knowledge of the girl
- is clearly distressed when the fact of the girl's death is fully realised
- does not blame the girl for what happened between them
- stresses the girl's good points
- shows care and compassion in his tone
- recognises how important he became to the girl
- admits she behaved better than he did.

CHECKPOINT 6, page 26

- Sheila admits that she disliked Gerald after his reactions to her own confession and her realisation that he had had a relationship with the girl.
- She says she now respects him more and acknowledges that he has been honest.
- She accepts that his motives were originally good ones and she recognises that by revealing their secrets each now sees the other in a new light.

CHECKPOINT 7, page 29

- The father is described as being young.
- He is 'silly and wild' (Act Two, p. 46) and we have seen Eric being silly at the dinner party.
- He drinks too much and, according to Mrs Birling, is a 'drunken young idler' (Act Two, p. 48).
- He comes from a different social class from the girl's.

CHECKPOINT 8, page 29

- Mrs Birling talks down to Sheila and the Inspector and looks down on those, like the girl, who she thinks have got themselves in trouble.
- She calls the Inspector 'impertinent' (Act Two, p. 30).
- She speaks 'haughtily' (Act Two, p. 30), 'grandly' (p. 31) and 'sharply' (p. 32).
- She claims to have done nothing wrong and tries to pass the blame on to anyone other than herself.
- She says the girl has only herself to blame, concentrating on blame instead of helping someone in trouble.
- She says, of the father of the unborn child, 'If the girl's death is due to anybody, then it's due to him' (Act Two, p. 48).
- She admits to being prejudiced.

CHECKPOINT 9, page 37

- Sheila feels it makes no difference. She recognises that they have all done wrong. She feels that he was their inspector (that is, he inspected their behaviour), whether he was a police officer or not.
- Eric supports Sheila. He sees the need for them all to change their behaviour.
- Mr Birling thinks that if the Inspector is not a real police officer there is less chance of a scandal over their dealings with the girl. He foresees no scandal relating to the money stolen from the firm's office. He persuades himself it has all been 'an elaborate sell' (Act Three, p. 70), that is, a trick.
- Mrs Birling supports her husband. She feels that if the Inspector was an imposter then she has been right to behave as she has.
- Gerald is excited by the prospect that there has not been any official investigation. He appears to believe that the Inspector being a fake puts things right.

CHECKPOINT 10, page 39

- Sheila and Eric accept responsibility.
- They do not feel that anything has happened to relieve their guilt.
- They realise the seriousness of their actions; they have taken the Inspector's message to heart and are fearful of the consequence if his words are not listened to.
- They have an understanding that they need to change their behaviour in the future.
- J. B. Priestley uses these two as symbols of the hope for a better future that lies in a younger generation.

PROGRESS AND REVISION CHECK ANSWERS

PART TWO, pages 40–1

SECTION ONE: CHECK YOUR KNOWLEDGE

1. Gerald Croft

2. Mr Birling

3. by drinking disinfectant

4. to keep labour costs down

5. the Inspector/Inspector Goole

6. Mr Birling and Sheila

7. not to hide anything from the Inspector

8. Mrs Birling; she means 'lower class'

9. Sheila tells her mother and Gerald confirms it.

10. He met her in spring/'sometime in March' (p. 34) the previous year; the affair ended six months later/'the first week of September' (p. 38).

11. She kept a diary.

12. to offer help to 'women in distress' (p. 42)/ to offer help to women who need support

13. the father of the unborn child

14. November of the previous year

15. about fifty pounds

16. each of the Birlings and Gerald Croft

17. Chief Constable Colonel Roberts

18. Gerald Croft

19. 'fire and blood and anguish' (pp. 56, 71)

20. Mr Birling answers; Mrs Birling, Sheila, Eric and Gerald are also present.

SECTION TWO: CHECK YOUR UNDERSTANDING

Task 1

- Sheila is pleased to be engaged to Gerald when she first receives the ring: 'Now I feel really engaged' (p. 5).

- She returns the ring when she learns about Gerald's affair with Daisy Renton: 'She hands him the ring' (p 40).

- Gerald's affair and her own treatment of Eva Smith makes her feel that Gerald and she 'aren't the same people who sat down to dinner' (p. 40).

- Sheila learns the need for community responsibility. She refuses the ring again because she needs time to consider how this and Gerald's affair affects their relationship: 'It's too soon. I must think' (p. 72).

Task 2

Mr Birling's judgement is poor because:

- His view is that there will be no trouble with his workers: 'Don't worry. We've passed the worst of it' (p. 6). We know strikes followed in 1912.

- He believes that the future of industry is rosy. He believes that the *Titanic* is 'unsinkable' (p. 7), but we know that it sank in 1912.

- He doesn't think there will be a war. He says, 'there isn't a chance of war' (p. 6), but the First World War began in 1914.

- He thinks that in the more distant future prospects will be good: 'let's say, in 1940' (p. 7), but this is the time of the Second World War.

PART THREE, page 53

SECTION ONE: CHECK YOUR KNOWLEDGE

1. Eric Birling, Sheila Birling, Gerald Croft (Acto One, p. 2)

2. Eva Smith, Daisy Renton, Mrs Birling

3. She is cold, reserved and prim.

4. triumphant/jubilant/victorious (or similar)

5. It 'creates an impression of massiveness, solidity and purposefulness' (Act One, p. 11). He has a large, solid and determined appearance (or similar).

6 Edna, the maid

7 Alderman Meggarty

8 A maid (Edna) and a cook

9 Lord and Lady Croft

10 Chief Constable Colonel Roberts

SECTION TWO: CHECK YOUR UNDERSTANDING

- He questions by speaking 'carefully, weightily and has a disconcerting habit of looking hard at the person before actually speaking' (Act One, p. 11).
- He asks questions in a way that demands answers. He says to Mrs Birling, 'You're not telling me the truth' (Act Two, p. 41).
- He begins by questioning politely: 'I'd like some information if you don't mind' (Act One, p. 11).
- He becomes increasingly forceful to gain control of the situation. He says to Mr Birling, 'Don't stammer and yammer at me again man' (Act Two, p. 46).

PART FOUR, page 62

SECTION ONE: CHECK YOUR KNOWLEDGE

1 Sheila, Eric

2 Mr Birling

3 The play returns to where it started, as it through a shift in time.

4 Mr Birling

5 at the celebratory dinner before the Inspector arrives

6 romantic love, family love, lust, universal love

7 Brumley

8 'An industrial city in the North Midlands.'

9 'An evening in spring, 1912'

10 when Inspector Goole enters

SECTION TWO: CHECK YOUR UNDERSTANDING

- According to the stage directions, Priestley wants to create the typical suburban dining room of a 'prosperous manufacturer' which has 'good solid furniture' (Act One, p. 1).
- The Birlings want to present an image of solidity and respectability, like their furniture.
- The stage directions also indicate 'white tie and tails' (Act One, p. 1) are to be worn, which is formal evening dress.
- The formal evening dress establishes the idea of tradition and correctness.

PART FIVE, page 69

SECTION ONE: CHECK YOUR KNOWLEDGE

1 voice

2 euphemism

3 rhetoric

4 morality play

5 'a chain of events'

6 form

7 structure

8 backstory

9 monologue

10 character trait

SECTION TWO: CHECK YOUR UNDERSTANDING

- There is a strong plot with links of cause and effect.
- There are revelations in which documents are often important.
- There is a backstory.
- There is a return to normality at the end.

MARK SCHEME

POINTS YOU COULD HAVE MADE

J. B. Priestley explores love from a wide variety of perspectives:

- **Romantic love** is shown in Sheila and Gerald's engagement and the ring is a symbol of love.
- Sheila's love is depicted in her broken speech 'Oh – it's wonderful! Oh –darling' (p. 5).
- Sheila's statement about she and Gerald no longer being 'the same people' (p. 40) questions whether their love was **true love**.
- Gerald's feelings for Daisy Renton sprung from **pity**, a kind of love.

- Daisy Renton's feelings for Gerald appear to have been a mix of love and **gratitude** since she was 'intensely grateful' (p. 37) for Gerald's help.
- Eric's reference to his meeting with Daisy Renton when he was drunk and 'when a chap easily turns nasty' (p. 52) reveals **lust** rather than love.
- The Birlings' **marriage** shows them united in their opinions – a kind of love.
- Mr and Mrs Birling are not demonstrative, revealing a lack of **affection**.
- Inspector Goole preaches **charity**/love for one's fellow human when he says, 'We are members of one body' (p. 56).

GENERAL SKILLS

Make a judgement about your level based on the points you made (above) and the skills you showed.

Level	Key elements	Spelling, punctuation and grammar	Tick your level
Very high	**Very well-structured answer which gives a rounded and convincing viewpoint.** You use very detailed analysis of the writer's methods and effects on the reader, using precise references which are fluently woven into what you say. You draw inferences, consider more than one perspective or angle, including the context where relevant, and make interpretations about the text as a whole.	You spell and punctuate with consistent accuracy, and use a very wide range of vocabulary and sentence structures to achieve effective control of meaning.	
Good to High	**A thoughtful, detailed response with well-chosen references.** At the top end, you address all aspects of the task in a clearly expressed way, and examine key aspects in detail. You are beginning to consider implications, explore alternative interpretations or ideas; at the top end, you do this fairly regularly and with some confidence.	You spell and punctuate with considerable accuracy, and use a considerable range of vocabulary and sentence structures to achieve general control of meaning.	
Mid	**A consistent response with clear understanding of the main ideas shown.** You use a range of references to support your ideas and your viewpoint is logical and easy to follow. Some evidence of commenting on writers' effects, though more needed.	You spell and punctuate with reasonable accuracy, and use a reasonable range of vocabulary and sentence structures.	
Lower	**Some relevant ideas but an inconsistent and rather simple response in places.** You show you have understood the task and you make some points to support what you say, but the evidence is not always well chosen. Your analysis is a bit basic and you do not comment in much detail on the writer's methods.	Your spelling and punctuation is inconsistent and your vocabulary and sentence structures are both limited. Some of these make your meaning unclear.	